THE
BENGHAZI
REPORT

Review of the Terrorist Attacks on U.S. Facilities
in Benghazi, Libya, September 11–12, 2012

U.S. SENATE SELECT COMMITTEE ON
INTELLIGENCE

INTRODUCTION BY
ROGER STONE

SKYHORSE PUBLISHING

Skyhorse Publishing books may be purchased in bulk at special discounts for sales promotion, corporate gifts, fund-raising, or educational purposes. Special editions can also be created to specifications. For details, contact the Special Sales Department, Skyhorse Publishing, 307 West 36th Street, 11th Floor, New York, NY 10018 or info@skyhorsepublishing.com.

Skyhorse® and Skyhorse Publishing® are registered trademarks of Skyhorse Publishing, Inc.®, a Delaware corporation.

Visit our website at www.skyhorsepublishing.com.

10 9 8 7 6 5 4 3 2 1

Library of Congress Cataloging-in-Publication Data is available on file.

ISBN: 978-1-62914-811-3

Printed in the United States of America

Contents

Why Benghazi Makes a Difference

AN INTRODUCTION BY ROGER STONE

This is the report that Hillary Clinton doesn't want you to read. This report by the U.S. Senate Select Committee on Intelligence contradicts a strained, page-one effort by the *New York Times* to exonerate then–Secretary of State Hillary Clinton for responsibility in the attacks on the American facility in Benghazi. In short, it is a report every American should read.

The release of the report on the September 11, 2012, attacks on the U.S. Department of State Temporary Mission Facility and CIA "Annex" in Benghazi, after numerous hearings, and despite significant resistance from the State Department and other executive branch agencies, substantiated a number of the criticisms leveled by Congress at President Obama and Secretary Clinton in the months following the attacks. The report's findings alone show a bipartisan consensus regarding the culpability of State Department officials including, but not limited to, Undersecretary of State for Management Patrick F. Kennedy, Deputy Assistant Secretary for International Programs Charlene Lamb, and ultimately Secretary Clinton herself.

The report, whose eighteen findings are generally commendable for their lack of bias (save for #9, which punts on the issues surrounding the executive branch talking points issued in the days following the attacks), not only takes aim at the Clinton-led State Department, though their fault was certainly the most spectacular, but also critiques other aspects of the executive branch. Finding numbers 4, 9, 10, 11, and 14 all involve significant failings from the various intelligence agencies, including the CIA, the FBI, the State Department's Bureau of Intelligence and Research, and the office of the Director of National Intelligence. Additionally, the committee found that the U.S. military under the direction of General Martin E. Dempsey failed to ensure that any U.S.

military assets were situated to intervene in support of U.S. operations within an acceptable time period. The failure of all these agencies and departments illustrates a failure of leadership at the highest levels of the administration.

However, it is impossible to read the committee's report without feeling anger, disgust, and contempt for those individuals at the highest echelons of the State Department who were at best incompetent, and at worse willfully negligent in protecting their employees. Employees who, had their superiors shown the least bit of interest in following their own already-established procedures, should never have remained in Benghazi through the end of the preceding summer. As is noted in finding #5, State Department officials overseeing the temporary mission for the Bureau of Near Eastern Affairs were aware that in the months preceding the attacks there had been *at least* twenty major security incidents involving "the Mission Facility, international organizations, and third party nationals." They were further aware that these multiple incidents crossed existing "tripwires" that should have, at the very least, ensured that far fewer personnel would remain in the facility—if any at all.

Further, the committee's findings illustrate a State Department whose leadership was far more concerned with the political "optics" of reinforcing the Benghazi facility than ensuring that the American citizens and allies working there were doing so in a safe environment. Vice-Chairman Chambliss, in the additional views of the minority appended to the report, reports that Deputy Assistant Secretary Lamb responded to requests to provide additional security agents for the DoS facilities in Libya by arguing it would be "embarrassing" to provide more agents than were in both Yemen and Pakistan—an argument she made despite knowing that unlike the facilities in Sanaa and Islamabad, the Benghazi facility was not up to the State Department's own security standards. Ms. Lamb, who despite losing her position was amazingly not drummed out of the State Department by Secretary Clinton, even informed then–Regional Security Officer Eric Nordstrom that she would not approve additional security personnel because "this is a political game."

The report also discusses, at length, the disparity between the response from State Department officials to the growing threat in Benghazi and that of the CIA for their response to threats to their Benghazi facility. Despite repeated petitions to upgrade the physical security of the facility, whose existence at a substandard physical location would have required authorization from Secretary Clinton herself, the extent of those upgrades were to be largely cosmetic—heightening the perimeter wall, and installing concrete Jersey barriers.

The internal State Department review of the attacks, cited by the committee, states that "[the facility] included a weak and very extended perimeter, an incomplete interior fence, no mantraps and unhardened entry gates and doors. Benghazi was also severely under-resourced with regard to weapons, ammunition, [non-lethal deterrents] and fire safety equipment, including escape masks." In a quote that could be an amusing tale of bureaucratic incompetence under other circumstances, the report notes, "the Mission facility had received additional surveillance cameras, but they *remained uninstalled because the State Department had not yet sent out the technical team necessary to install them* [emphasis added]. In addition . . . the camera monitor in the local guard force booth next to the main gate was inoperable on the day of the attacks due to a needed repair by a technical team."

By way of comparison, the security improvements made to the CIA Annex, while redacted, take up an entire page of the report—and while the exact security procedures the CIA utilized remain classified, it seems a safe bet that *their* security cameras were both installed and operating on the day of the attacks. This failure to adequately protect the Benghazi facility belongs not just to Ms. Lamb, but also to Undersecretary Kennedy, who turned down offers of Department of Defense security personnel support for State Department operations in Libya from Lt. General Robert Neller, USMC Director of Operations, J3, the Joint Staff.

Finally, while the facts of the investigation presented do not press into the root causes of the inaccurate talking points released in the days following the attacks (that task, partisan as it is, was left for the "additional views" following the report), the report states in no uncertain terms that there was no protest at the mission facility before or during the attacks. Furthermore, while again refusing to assign motive, the report notes what all can agree, that following the initial release of the faulty talking points the administration was indefensibly slow to correct the glaring errors. Despite the official report's refusing to make a definitive statement regarding the reasoning behind the composition of those talking points, the Committee Minority's view that this remains one of the open questions relating to the attacks rings true. This fact, too, reflects the extraordinary hubris and lack of accountability of high-ranking administration officials.

There will be those who will claim that the failures of the officials cited above, and of numerous others in the following report, do not amount to a failure at the top. These apologists for Secretary Clinton and President Obama point elatedly to a December 28, 2013, in-depth report from *New York Times*

Cairo bureau chief David Kirkpatrick. Kirkpatrick's report is done a disservice by his paper's editorial board, which in an editorial published two days later blithely accuses congressional Republicans of "conspiracy-mongering and an obsessive effort to discredit President Obama and former Secretary of State Hillary Rodham Clinton." It further concludes that Mr. Kirkpatrick's report is "a reminder that the Benghazi tragedy represents a gross intelligence failure, something that has largely been overlooked in the public debate." This blatantly partisan assertion should have been obvious even to the *Times* editors based on Kirkpatrick's reporting alone.

Kirkpatrick's reporting on the issue of intelligence appreciations of the threat posed shows excerpts from Ambassador Stevens's diary, which includes the following passage: "[There is a] security vacuum. . . . Militias are power on the ground. Dicey conditions, including car bombs, attacks on consulate . . . Islamist 'hit list' in Benghazi. Me targeted on a prominent Islamist website (no more off compound jogging) . . . *Never ending security threats* [emphasis added]." While Kirkpatrick did not have access to the diplomatic cables and email correspondence that are cited in the Senate report, in which Stevens and others repeatedly asked for additional security, even the liberal *Times* editorial board should have recognized that a man of Ambassador Stevens's intelligence would not simply note the threats to the security of himself and his staff without requesting additional protection. Had the *Times* editors read even Mr. Kirkpatrick's imperfect report they should have recognized the appropriate message of their editorial was not to blindly support the president and Secretary Clinton, but rather to demand that the obvious security questions be answered.

Barring the glaringly obvious question of why American personnel at the State Department facility were left with inadequate protection, particularly in comparison to the CIA facility, the *Times* editors could also have sought answers about why the perpetrators of the murders of four Americans have yet to be brought to justice. Kirkpatrick's report notes that "by last summer . . . [the United States] formally asked the Libyan government to arrest Mr. Abu Khattala, along with a dozen others." Not surprisingly, the Libyan government, such as it is, closed ranks and has thus far refused to act on the matter—whether this is because it is unable or simply unwilling to do so is irrelevant. Sensibly, according to Kirkpatrick, "the United States military also prepared a plan to capture him on its own, pending Presidential approval. . . . But the administration held back, fearing that unilateral military action could set off a backlash that would undermine the fragile Libyan government."

The revelation that the U.S. government has made an affirmative choice not to bring the killers of four Americans to justice is disturbing and unconscionable. Mr. Kirkpatrick's assertion is not confirmed in the Senate report; however, logic would argue in favor of its truth. Let us reflect on how President Obama famously ordered the mission—violating the airspace of nuclear-armed Pakistan—that ultimately led to the killing of Osama bin Laden. The very same president, on whose authority unmanned drones have violated the airspace of numerous countries thousands of times, has evidently gotten cold feet when it comes to apprehending the mastermind of the killing of Ambassador Stevens and three other Americans.

Instead of asking the two most obvious questions raised by Kirkpatrick's report, the *Times* focuses on driving home a point that the Senate report finds cannot be concluded based on the available evidence. According to Kirkpatrick's reporting, oftentimes citing individuals who were involved with the attacks, the impetus for the attacks was an inflammatory video posted on YouTube criticizing the prophet Muhammad. According to the Senate report's finding #14, "some intelligence suggests the attacks were likely put together in short order, following that day's violent protests in Cairo against an inflammatory video." While for the Senate this statement serves as a warning that America's enemies can move swiftly to seize opportunities, to the *Times* and other liberal apologists the video serves to liberate both President Obama and Secretary Clinton from responsibility, for reasons that are, at best, unclear—the president and secretary being those individuals most responsible for ensuring that American consular staff are safe from such attacks.

To apologists for Secretary Clinton and President Obama, despite the two having oversight authority for the placement of the individuals with direct responsibility for the protection of the temporary mission facility in their positions, the argument is that the government bureaucracy is vast and no two people can keep watch over it in its entirety. This point will be argued vehemently, with no apparent appreciation for irony, by those same individuals who have in years past criticized President Bush for the failures of Michael D. Brown as FEMA director. It is true that President Obama cannot be in all places at all times. However, his influence is shown in those whom he chooses to trust with important government posts. The failures of Undersecretary Kennedy, Deputy Assistant Secretary Lamb, Secretary Clinton, and General Dempsey are the failures of the man who put the nation's trust in them.

The defenders of the president must twist, or downright ignore, many of the facts of the buildup to, actions during, and investigation of the attacks in order to achieve anything approximating a logically coherent defense. Such an argument generally chooses to attack Republican members of Congress for "fear-mongering" or being "conspiracy theorists" to overwhelm the large body of evidence incriminating President Obama and Secretary Clinton.

However, the facts of the case stand on their own. In the months leading up to the attack, both the State Department and CIA received reports from their agents on the ground suggesting an increased danger to their activities. The CIA acted to increase security; the State Department ignored pleas from its employees and did nothing of any great effect. Upon the revelation that its facilities were woefully below standard, the State Department sought to shift blame for the failure onto the intelligence community. Finally, following the attacks, and despite having actionable intelligence on the identities and locations of the perpetrators, the Obama administration has punted on bringing the instigators to justice.

The following report is damning in presenting the case that President Obama and Secretary Clinton, as well as a number of others, helped ensure the events of September 11, 2012, could happen, and that when in progress the attacks could not be adequately handled. Following the conclusion of the attacks, they too were among those deceiving Congress, delaying investigations, and protecting those guilty of making the attacks possible. It is my hope that by reading the contents of this report the American people can come to see for themselves the shocking failures that have remained persistently unaddressed by the president and his administration.

An overriding tenet of American foreign policy in the era of global terrorism has been to do whatever possible to ensure the protection of American nationals in high-risk areas, and failing that, to bring the perpetrators of terror to justice. This report proves that while the administration might talk a big game, when it comes to Benghazi it has shown itself to be incompetent, untrustworthy, and unwilling to act.

When asked about her role in the death of Americans in Benghazi, Hillary Clinton asked, "What *difference* at this point *does it make?*" I say it *does* make a difference and the contents of this report outline why Mrs. Clinton has neither the judgment, nor the experience or veracity to be Commander-in-Chief.

U.S. Senate Select Committee on
INTELLIGENCE

REVIEW

of the

TERRORIST ATTACKS ON U.S. FACILITIES

IN BENGHAZI, LIBYA, SEPTEMBER 11-12, 2012

together with

ADDITIONAL VIEWS

January 15, 2014

SENATE SELECT COMMITTEE ON INTELLIGENCE

United States Senate

113th Congress

SSCI Review of the Terrorist Attacks on U.S. Facilities in Benghazi, Libya, September 11-12, 2012

I. PURPOSE OF THIS REPORT

The purpose of this report is to review the September 11-12, 2012, terrorist attacks against two U.S. facilities in Benghazi, Libya. This review by the Senate Select Committee on Intelligence (hereinafter "SSCI" or "the Committee") focuses primarily on the analysis by and actions of the Intelligence Community (IC) leading up to, during, and immediately following the attacks. The report also addresses, as appropriate, other issues about the attacks as they relate to the Department of Defense (DoD) and Department of State (State or State Department).

It is important to acknowledge at the outset that diplomacy and intelligence collection are inherently risky, and that all risk cannot be eliminated. Diplomatic and intelligence personnel work in high-risk locations all over the world to collect information necessary to prevent future attacks against the United States and our allies. Between 1998 (the year of the terrorist attacks against the U.S. Embassies in Kenya and Tanzania) and 2012, 273 significant attacks were carried out against U.S. diplomatic facilities and personnel.[1] The need to place personnel in high-risk locations carries significant vulnerabilities for the United States. The Committee intends for this report to help increase security and reduce the risks to our personnel serving overseas and to better explain what happened before, during, and after the attacks.

II. THE COMMITTEE'S REVIEW[2]

Hearings, Briefings, and Meetings: The Committee began its initial review of the September 11, 2012, terrorist attacks against the U.S facilities in Benghazi, Libya, on September 13, 2012, which transitioned into a formal review a few

---

[1] U.S. Department of State, Bureau of Diplomatic Security, *Significant Attacks Against U.S. Diplomatic Facilities and Personnel, 1998-2012*, revised July 2013. This report also states on page i: "This information is not an all-inclusive compilation; rather, it is a reasonably comprehensive listing of significant attacks."

[2] The Committee notes that the IC, State, and DoD provided the Committee with hundreds of key documents throughout this review, although sometimes with a significant amount of resistance, especially from State. This lack of cooperation unnecessarily hampered the Committee's review.

weeks later. This report and our findings and recommendations are based upon the extensive work conducted by Committee Members and staff during this review, including the following hearings, briefings, and meetings (which included interviews of U.S. personnel on the ground during the attacks):

- Three Committee oversight hearings with witnesses from the Office of the Director of National Intelligence (ODNI), National Counterterrorism Center (NCTC), Central Intelligence Agency (CIA), Federal Bureau of Investigation (FBI), State, and DoD;

- Two Committee briefings with David Petraeus—one while he was CIA Director and one after his resignation;

- Three Committee briefings with Robert Litt, ODNI General Counsel, regarding the issue of the CIA Talking Points;

- Four on-the record Member and staff meetings with:

  1. Gregory Hicks, Deputy Chief of Mission (DCM) in Tripoli during the attacks;[3]

  2. Mark Thompson, Acting Deputy Assistant Secretary for Counterterrorism at the State Department;

  3. Eric Nordstrom, former Regional Security Officer (RSO) in Libya; and

  4. the former CIA Chief of Base in Benghazi who was at the Annex on the night of the attacks; and

- At least 17 other staff briefings and meetings, including interviews of U.S. Government security personnel on the ground in Benghazi the night of the attacks.

---

[3] Mr. Hicks met with Committee staff, without Senators, in a follow-up session. *See* SSCI Transcript, *Staff Interview of Gregory Hicks*, June 19, 2003.

Documents and Video Reviewed: The Committee reviewed: (1) thousands of intelligence reports and internal documents (including e-mails, cables, etc.) which were provided by the IC, the State Department, and DoD; (2) written responses to Committee questions for the record; (3) numerous open-source materials; and (4) surveillance videos related to the attacks.

III. DESCRIPTION OF THE SEPTEMBER 11-12, 2012, ATTACKS

The sequence of events in Benghazi on the night of September 11, 2012, and the morning of September 12, 2012, have been widely described in media and other reports. There were effectively at least three different attacks against U.S. facilities in fewer than eight hours. Understanding the evolution and the sequence of attacks is important to provide the context in which Americans in Benghazi and Tripoli and U.S. officials in Washington, D.C., evaluated events as they unfolded and formulated operational and policy responses. Below are the key details about the three attacks.

1. Attack on the U.S. Temporary Mission Facility at Approximately 9:40 p.m.

At approximately 9:40 p.m. Benghazi time, on September 11, 2012, dozens of attackers easily gained access to the U.S. Temporary Mission Facility (hereinafter "the TMF," "the Mission facility," or "the Mission compound") by scaling and then opening the front vehicle gate.[4] Over the course of the entire attack on the TMF, at least 60 different attackers entered the U.S. compound and can be seen on the surveillance video recovered from the Mission facility.[5] The attackers moved unimpeded throughout the compound, entering and exiting buildings at will.

After entering the Mission facility, the attackers used diesel fuel to set fire to the barracks/guard house of the Libyan 17th February Brigade militia, which served as a security force provided by the host nation for the Mission compound, and then proceeded towards the main buildings of the compound.[6] A Diplomatic Security (DS) agent working in the Tactical Operations Center (TOC) of the Mission

---

[4] SSCI Transcript, *Hearing on the Attacks in Benghazi*, November 15, 2012, p. 24.
[5] James R. Clapper, Director of National Intelligence, *Joint Statement for the Record, SSCI Hearing on the Attacks in Benghazi*, November 15, 2012, p. 3.
[6] Ibid.

facility immediately activated the Imminent Danger Notification System.[7] He also alerted the CIA personnel stationed at the nearby CIA Annex (hereinafter "the Annex"), the Libyan 17th February Brigade, the U.S. Embassy in Tripoli, and the Diplomatic Security Command Center (DSCC) in Washington, D.C.[8]

There were five DS agents at the Mission compound that night. Two had traveled from Tripoli with U.S. Ambassador to Libya Christopher Stevens (who was staying at the Mission compound in Benghazi), and three others were assigned to the Mission facility. In addition to the five DS agents on duty, there were three armed members of the Libyan 17th February Brigade militia, three Libyan National Police officers, and five unarmed members of a local security team contracted through a British company, Blue Mountain Group, who were guarding the Mission facility that night. In addition, six armed CIA security personnel (plus an interpreter) operating out of the nearby Annex were able to respond quickly after receiving word of the attack.

After the DS agent in the Tactical Operations Center at the Temporary Mission Facility alerted the Annex security team that the TMF was under attack at approximately 9:40 p.m., the Chief of Base called the ███████████████████ ███████████████, "who advised that he would immediately deploy a █████████ ████████ force to provide assistance," according to a September 19, 2012, cable that provided the joint CIA Station/Base report on the events surrounding the September 11-12 attacks.[9]

Two armored vehicles were prepared so the security team could respond from the Annex. Approximately 20-25 minutes after the first call came into the Annex that the Temporary Mission Facility was under attack, a security team left the Annex for the Mission compound. In footage taken from the Annex's security cameras, the security team can be observed departing the CIA Annex at 10:03 p.m. Benghazi time. During the period between approximately 9:40 p.m. and 10:03 p.m. Benghazi time, the Chief of Base and security team members attempted to secure assistance and heavy weapons (such as .50 caliber truck-mounted machine guns) from the 17th February Brigade and other militias that had been assisting the United States.[10] Then, the team drove to the Mission facility and made their way

---

[7] NCTC and FBI, *The 11-12 September Attacks on US Facilities in Benghazi*, November 13, 2012, p. 3.
[8] Ibid.
[9] E-mail from ████████████████ to ████████████, "Fw: Subject: Eyes Only – Tripoli Station and Benghazi Base Report on Events of 11-12 September," containing CIA TRIPOLI 27900, September 19, 2012, p. 2.
[10] Classified Report of the Department of State Accountability Review Board (ARB), December 18, 2012, p. 27.

onto the Mission compound in the face of enemy fire, arriving in the vicinity of the compound at approximately 10:10 p.m. Benghazi time.[11] The Committee explored claims that there was a "stand down" order given to the security team at the Annex. Although some members of the security team expressed frustration that they were unable to respond more quickly to the Mission compound,[12] the Committee found no evidence of intentional delay or obstruction by the Chief of Base or any other party.[13]

Meanwhile, a DS agent secured Ambassador Stevens and State Department Information Management Officer Sean Smith in the "safe area" of the main building of the Mission facility (Building C). The attackers used diesel fuel to set the main building ablaze and thick smoke rapidly filled the entire structure. According to testimony of the Director of the NCTC, the DS agent began leading the Ambassador and Mr. Smith toward the emergency escape window to escape the smoke.[14] Nearing unconsciousness himself, the agent opened the emergency escape window and crawled out. He then realized he had become separated from the Ambassador and Sean Smith in the smoke, so he reentered and searched the building multiple times.[15] The DS agent, suffering from severe smoke inhalation, climbed a ladder to the roof where he radioed the other DS agents for assistance and attempted unsuccessfully to ventilate the building by breaking a skylight.[16]

Other DS agents went to retrieve their M-4 carbine assault rifles from Building B when the attack began. When they attempted to return to the main building (Building C) to help protect the Ambassador, they encountered armed attackers and decided to return to Building B to take cover rather than open fire. They eventually regrouped, made their way to a nearby armored vehicle, and then drove over to assist the agent on the roof of Building C searching for the

---

[11] NCTC and FBI, *The 11-12 September Attacks on US Facilities in Benghazi*, November 13, 2012, p. 4; E-mail from CIA Office of Congressional Affairs (OCA) staff to Staff Director, House Permanent Select Committee on Intelligence (HPSCI), et al., "Background Points used on 1 Nov," November 2, 2012, p. 1.

[12] SSCI Memorandum for the Record, "Staff Briefing and Secure Video Teleconference (SVTC) with CIA Benghazi Survivors," June 27, 2013.

[13] According to informal notes obtained from the CIA, the security team left for the Annex without the formal approval of the Chief of Base, *see* attachments to e-mail from CIA staff ███████ to CIA staff ████ ███████, September 23, 2012. However, a Memorandum for the Record prepared by the Deputy Chief of Base specifically states that the Chief "authorized the move" and the Chief told the Committee: "We launched our QRF [Quick Reaction Force] as soon as possible down to the State [Department] compound." ███████████, Memorandum for the Record, "Events of 11-12 SEP 2012 at Benghazi Base, Libya," September 19, 2012, p. 1; and SSCI Transcript, *Member and Staff Interview of former Chief of Base*, December 20, 2012, p. 3.

[14] SSCI Transcript, *Hearing on the Attacks in Benghazi*, November 15, 2012, pp. 27-29.

[15] NCTC and FBI, *The 11-12 September Attacks on US Facilities in Benghazi*, November 13, 2012, p. 4.

[16] Unclassified Report of the ARB, December 18, 2012, p. 22.

Ambassador and Mr. Smith. After numerous attempts, they found Mr. Smith, who was deceased.[17] The DS agents did not fire a single shot that night during the attack on the Temporary Mission Facility, according to testimony before the Committee.[18]

Outside the compound, the security team asked 17th February Brigade members to "provide cover" for them to advance to the gate of the Temporary Mission Facility with gun trucks. The 17th February Brigade members refused, saying they preferred to negotiate with the attackers instead. Eventually, the security team initiated their plan of assault on the Mission compound. Some members of the 17th February Brigade "jump[ed] into the vehicle" and "a few 17 Feb members follow[ed] behind on foot to support the team," according to the informal CIA notes provided to the Committee.[19]

When the security team from the Annex arrived on the grounds of the Mission facility, "the officers exchanged fire with the attackers."[20] The CIA security team carried

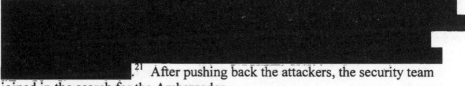

[21] After pushing back the attackers, the security team joined in the search for the Ambassador.

At approximately 11:10 p.m. Benghazi time, an unarmed, unmanned DoD Predator surveillance aircraft, which had been diverted approximately one hour earlier by U.S. Africa Command (AFRICOM) from another intelligence collection mission in eastern Libya, arrived over the Mission compound and soon after

---

[17] Charlene Lamb, Deputy Assistant Secretary of State for International Programs, Bureau of Diplomatic Security, U.S. Department of State, *Statement for the Record,* House Committee on Oversight and Government Reform (HOGR), *Hearing on the Security Failures of Benghazi,* October 10, 2012, p. 6.

[18] SSCI Transcript, *Hearing on Security Issues at Benghazi and Threats to U.S. Intelligence and Diplomatic Personnel and Facilities Worldwide Since the Attacks,* December 4, 2012, p. 67. However, on page 47 of its classified report, the ARB concluded: "While none of the five DS agents discharged their weapons, the Board concluded that this was a sound tactical decision, given the overwhelming degree to which they were outgunned and outnumbered: A decision to discharge their weapons may well have resulted in more American deaths that night, without saving lives. The multiple trips that DS agents and Annex security team members made into a burning, smoke-filled building showed readiness to risk life and limb to save others."

[19] *See* attachments to e-mail from CIA staff ████████ to CIA staff ████████, September 23, 2012.

[20] CIA TRIPOLI 27900, September 19, 2012, p. 3.

[21] SSCI Transcript, *Benghazi Follow Up with Staff,* May 22, 2013, p. 72.

detected a roadblock several blocks east of the Mission facility.[22] During this time, State and CIA personnel re-entered the burning compound numerous times in an attempt to locate Ambassador Stevens, but to no avail. Under the impression that the Ambassador "had already been taken from that compound and that he'd been kidnapped," the leader of the Annex security team decided that U.S. personnel needed to evacuate to the Annex for their safety.[23] DS special agents agreed with the decision to evacuate.

Together, CIA and DS security personnel made a final search for the Ambassador before leaving for the Annex in two separate armored vehicles.[24] One vehicle encountered heavy fire as it ran a roadblock several blocks east of the Mission compound.[25] Both vehicles were eventually able to make their way to the Annex, which was approximately two kilometers away. By approximately 11:30 p.m. Benghazi time, all U.S. personnel, except for the missing Ambassador, had departed the Mission compound.[26] Mr. Smith's remains were also taken to the Annex.

2. Attack on the CIA Annex from Approximately 11:56 p.m. until 1:00 a.m.

The U.S. personnel evacuating the Mission facility were followed by some of the attackers to the CIA Annex nearby.[27] Although officially under cover, the Annex was known by some in Benghazi as an American facility. At approximately 11:56 p.m. Benghazi time, sporadic arms fire and rocket-propelled grenades (RPGs) were fired at the Annex.[28] Over the next hour, the Annex took sporadic small arms fire and RPG rounds, the security team returned fire, and the attackers dispersed.[29] It is likely U.S. personnel injured or possibly killed some of the attackers during the exchange of fire. "[T]hey probably took casualties. I'm quite sure they took casualties," according to the Chief of Base.[30]

---

[22] DoD, *Timeline of Department of Defense Actions on September 11-12, 2012*, April 1, 2013, p. 1.
[23] SSCI Transcript, *Member and Staff Interview of former Chief of Base*, December 20, 2012, p. 5; SSCI Transcript, *Hearing on the Attacks in Benghazi*, November 15, 2012, p. 35.
[24] HOGR Transcript, *Hearing on the Security Failures of Benghazi*, October 10, 2012, p. 32; NCTC and FBI, *The 11-12 September Attacks on U.S. Facilities in Benghazi*, November 13, 2012, pp. 4-5.
[25] SSCI Transcript, *Hearing on the Attacks in Benghazi*, November 15, 2012, p. 35.
[26] NCTC and FBI, *The 11-12 September Attacks on US Facilities in Benghazi*, November 13, 2012, p. 5.
[27] SSCI Transcript, *Member and Staff Interview of former Chief of Base*, December 20, 2012, p. 60.
[28] NCTC and FBI, *The 11-12 September Attacks on US Facilities in Benghazi*, November 13, 2012, p. 5.
[29] E-mail from CIA OCA staff to Staff Director, HPSCI, et al., "Background Points used on 1 Nov," November 2, 2012, p. 1.
[30] SSCI Transcript, *Member and Staff Interview of former Chief of Base*, December 20, 2012, p. 61.

At approximately 1:15 a.m. Benghazi time, a seven-man reinforcement team of additional U.S. security personnel from Tripoli landed at the Benghazi airport and began to negotiate with the local Libyan militias for transportation and a security convoy.[31] Upon learning Ambassador Stevens was still missing and that the situation at the Annex had calmed, the team focused on locating the Ambassador and trying to obtain information on the security situation at the Benghazi Medical Center where he was said to be.[32] An individual at the hospital made calls from the Ambassador's cell phone to numbers stored in the phone, including to some numbers in Tripoli and to one of the RSOs. After an exchange of calls between the individual in possession of Stevens's phone and some of the Americans, the Americans became concerned that the caller could be luring U.S. personnel into an ambush at the hospital and concluded it was too risky to go to the hospital.

After more than three hours of negotiations and communications with Libyan officials who expressed concern about the security situation at the hospital, the Libyan government arranged for the Libyan Shield Militia to provide transportation and an armed escort from the airport.[33] After learning that Ambassador Stevens was almost certainly dead and that the security situation at the hospital was uncertain, the team opted to go to the Annex to support the other U.S. personnel.[34] The security team from Tripoli departed the airport for the Annex at approximately 4:30 a.m. Benghazi time.[35]

3. Attack on the CIA Annex at Approximately 5:15 a.m.

At approximately 5:00 a.m. Benghazi time, the security team from Tripoli arrived at the Annex just moments before the third attack that night. At approximately 5:15 a.m. Benghazi time, mortar rounds began to hit the Annex. Two security officers, Tyrone Woods and Glen Doherty, were killed when they took direct mortar fire as they engaged the enemy from the roof of the Annex.[36] The mortar fire also seriously injured one other security officer and one DS special

---

[31] NCTC and FBI, *The 11-12 September Attacks on US Facilities in Benghazi,* November 13, 2012, p. 6.
[32] E-mail from CIA OCA staff to Staff Director, HPSCI, et al., "Background Points used on 1 Nov," November 2, 2012, p. 1.
[33] SSCI Transcript, *Benghazi Follow Up with Staff,* May 22, 2013, p. 34.
[34] E-mail from CIA OCA staff to Staff Director, HPSCI, et al., "Background Points used on 1 Nov," November 2, 2012, p. 1.
[35] SSCI Transcript, *Benghazi Follow Up with Staff,* May 22, 2013, p. 34.
[36] NCTC and FBI, *The 11-12 September Attacks on US Facilities in Benghazi,* November 13, 2012, p. 6.

agent, necessitating the evacuation of the Annex.[37] That attack lasted only 11 minutes, then dissipated.[38] The mortar fire was particularly accurate, demonstrating a lethal capability and sophistication that changed the dynamic on the ground that night. According to testimony by the Chief of Base, it was only after this third wave of attacks, when the mortars hit, that he decided it was necessary to evacuate the personnel from the Annex.[39]

Less than an hour later, a heavily-armed Libyan militia unit arrived to help evacuate the Annex of all U.S. personnel to the airport. The Ambassador's body, which had been secured by a local Libyan coordinating with the State Department, was also transported from the Benghazi Medical Center to the airport. By approximately 10:00 a.m. Benghazi time, all U.S. personnel and the bodies of the four dead Americans departed from Benghazi to Tripoli.[40]

IV. FINDINGS AND RECOMMENDATIONS

Warnings Before the Attacks and Failures to Provide Security

FINDING #1: In the months before the attacks on September 11, 2012, the IC provided ample strategic warning that the security situation in eastern Libya was deteriorating and that U.S. facilities and personnel were at risk in Benghazi.

The IC produced hundreds of analytic reports in the months preceding the September 11-12, 2012, attacks, providing strategic warning that militias and terrorist and affiliated groups had the capability and intent to strike U.S. and Western facilities and personnel in Libya. For example:

- On June 12, 2012, the Defense Intelligence Agency (DIA) produced a report entitled, "Libya: Terrorists Now Targeting U.S. and Western Interests." The report noted recent attacks against the U.S. Mission compound in Benghazi,

---

[37] SSCI Transcript, *Member and Staff Interview of former Chief of Base*, December 20, 2012, p. 42.
[38] E-mail from CIA OCA staff to Staff Director, HPSCI, et al., "Background Points used on 1 Nov," November 2, 2012, p. 1.
[39] SSCI Transcript, *Member and Staff Interview of former Chief of Base*, December 20, 2012, p. 42, in which the Chief of Base said: "Until the mortar attack, we were pretty comfortable that we could stave off any type of ground assault on the Annex."
[40] NCTC and FBI, *The 11-12 September Attacks on US Facilities in Benghazi*, November 13, 2012, p. 7.

the growing ties between al-Qa'ida (AQ) regional nodes and Libya-based terrorists, and stated: "We expect more anti-U.S. terrorist attacks in eastern Libya ▮▮▮▮▮▮▮▮▮▮▮▮, due to the terrorists' greater presence there....This will include terrorists conducting more ambush and IED [improvised explosive device] attacks as well as more threats against ▮▮▮▮▮▮▮▮▮▮▮▮▮▮▮ ."[41]

- On June 18, 2012, the Pentagon's Joint Staff produced a slide in its daily intelligence report entitled, "(U) Terrorism: Conditions Ripe for More Attacks, Terrorist Safe Haven in Libya." In the slide, the Joint Staff assessed: "▮▮▮▮▮▮▮ support will increase Libyan terrorist capability in the permissive post-revolution security environment. Attacks will also increase in number and lethality as terrorists connect with AQ associates in Libya. Areas of eastern Libya will likely become a safe haven by the end of 2012 ▮▮▮▮▮▮▮▮▮▮▮▮▮▮▮▮▮ ."[42]

- On July 2, 2012, DIA produced a report that discussed the founding of Ansar al-Sharia (AAS) entitled, ▮▮▮▮▮▮▮▮▮▮▮ The report stated: ▮▮▮▮▮

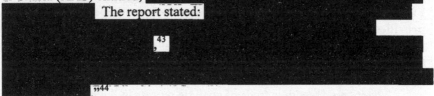

."[44]

- On July 6, 2012, CIA produced a report entitled, "Libya: Al-Qa'ida Establishing Sanctuary." In the report, CIA stated: "Al-Qa'ida-affiliated groups and associates are exploiting the permissive security environment in Libya to enhance their capabilities and expand their operational reach. This year, Muhammad Jamal's Egypt-based network, al-Qa'ida in the Arabian Peninsula (AQAP), and al-Qa'ida in the Lands of the Islamic Maghreb (AQIM) have conducted training, built communication networks, and

---

[41] DIA, "Libya: Terrorists Now Targeting U.S. and Western Interests," Defense Intelligence Report, June 12, 2012.
[42] Joint Staff, "Terrorism: Conditions Ripe for More Attacks, Terrorist Safe Haven in Libya," J-2 Intelligence Update, June 18, 2012.
[43] Qumu was released from Guantanamo Bay in 2007.
[44] DIA, "▮▮▮▮▮▮▮▮▮▮▮▮▮▮▮▮▮▮▮▮▮▮▮▮▮▮▮▮," Defense Intelligence Digest, July 2, 2012.

facilitated extremist travel across North Africa from their safe haven in parts of eastern Libya."[45]

- On August 19, 2012, the Pentagon's Joint Staff produced a slide in its daily intelligence report entitled, "(U) Libya: Terrorists to Increase Strength During Next Six Months." In the slide, the Joint Staff stated: "There are no near-term prospects for a reversal in the trend towards a terrorist safe haven in Libya, and areas of eastern Libya will likely become a broader safe haven by the end of 2012. The conditions in Libya will allow terrorists to increase attacks against Western and Libyan interests in the country, as well as attempt attacks in the region and possibly Europe in the next six months."[46]

- On September 5, 2012, AFRICOM produced a Theater Analysis Report entitled, "(U) Libya: Extremism in Libya Past, Present, and Future." The report contained a map showing how "███████████████ are actively exploiting the open operating environment in Libya." (The map is located in Appendix IV of this report). The report also noted: "Disarray in Libya's security services, and a likely focus by authorities on pursuit of Qadhafi loyalists is likely allowing jihadists in Libya freedom to recruit, train, and facilitate the movement of fighters and weapons. The threat to Western and U.S. interests and individuals remains high, particularly in northeast-Libya."[47]

- On September 7, 2012, DIA produced a report entitled, "███████████████████████ ███████████" that stated: "██████████

"[48]

FINDING #2: The State Department should have increased its security posture more significantly in Benghazi based on the deteriorating security situation on the ground and IC threat reporting on the prior attacks against

---

[45] CIA, "Libya: Al-Qa'ida Establishing Sanctuary," WIRe, July 6, 2012.

[46] Joint Staff, "Libya: Terrorists to Increase Strength During Next Six Months," J-2 Intelligence Update, August 19, 2012.

[47] United States Africa Command, "Libya: Extremism in Libya Past, Present, and Future," United States Africa Command Theater Analysis Report, September 5, 2012.

[48] DIA, "████████████████████████," Defense Intelligence Digest, September 7, 2012.

Westerners in Benghazi—including two incidents at the Temporary Mission Facility on April 6 and June 6, 2012.

State Department officials, including Ambassador Stevens, were aware of, and had regular access to, threat reporting on Libya. According to DCM Greg Hicks, he and Ambassador Stevens regularly read the intelligence coming out of the CIA and communicated with the █████████████████████████████, and other intelligence officials on a daily basis.[49] As part of this regular interaction, the Ambassador was provided with an intelligence "read book," which would include information on the security situation and terrorism issues. The read book was also supplied to the Embassy's RSO.[50]

As the Accountability Review Board found, there were at least 20 security incidents involving the Temporary Mission Facility, international organizations, non-governmental organizations, and third-country nationals and diplomats in the Benghazi area in the months leading up to the September 11, 2012, attacks.[51] The

[49] SSCI Transcript, *Member and Staff Interview of Gregory Hicks and Mark Thompson,* June 12, 2013, p. 39.
[50] SSCI Transcript, *Benghazi Follow Up with Staff,* May 22, 2013, p. 36.
[51] The 20 security incidents detailed in the unclassified report of the ARB on pages 15-16 are as follows:
- March 18, 2012—Armed robbery occurs at the British School in Benghazi.
- March 22, 2012—Members of a militia searching for a suspect fire their weapons near the U.S. Mission and attempt to enter.
- April 2, 2012—A British armored diplomatic vehicle is attacked after driving into a local protest; the vehicle was damaged but occupants uninjured.
- April 6, 2012—A gelatina bomb or "fish bomb" (traditional homemade explosive device used for fishing) is thrown over the Temporary Mission Facility's north wall.
- April 10, 2012—An IED (gelatina or dynamite stick) is thrown at the motorcade of the United Nations (UN) Special Envoy to Libya in Benghazi.
- April 26, 2012—The principal officer of the U.S. Mission is evacuated from the International Medical University (IMU) after a fistfight escalated to gunfire between Tripoli-based trade delegation security personnel and IMU security.
- April 27, 2012—Two South African nationals in Libya as part of a U.S.-funded weapons abatement, unexploded ordnance removal, and demining project are detained at gunpoint by militia, questioned, and released.
- May 22, 2012—Benghazi-based International Committee of the Red Cross (ICRC) building is struck by RPGs.
- May 28, 2012—A previously unknown organization, Omar Abdurrahman group, claims responsibility for the ICRC attack and issues a threat against the United States on social media sites.
- June 6, 2012—IED attack on the Temporary Mission Facility; the IED detonates with no injuries but blows a large hole in the compound's exterior wall. Omar Abdurrahman group makes an unsubstantiated claim of responsibility.
- June 8, 2012—Two hand grenades target a parked United Kingdom (UK) diplomatic vehicle in Sabha (800 km south of Benghazi).
- June 11, 2012—While in Benghazi, the British Ambassador's convoy is attacked with an RPG and possible AK-47s; two UK security officers are injured. The UK closes its mission in Benghazi the following day.

Intelligence Community reported on several of these incidents in finished intelligence products prior to the September 11, 2012, attacks, including:[52,53,54,55]

- April 6, 2012—A small IED was thrown over the wall of the Temporary Mission Facility.

- April 10, 2012—An explosive device was thrown at a convoy in Benghazi carrying the head of the UN mission to Libya.

- May 22, 2012—The ICRC building in Benghazi was attacked with RPGs. The Omar Abdul Rahman Brigade[56] claimed responsibility for the attack, according to press, social media, and other intelligence.

- June 6, 2012—An IED exploded near the main gate of the Mission facility in Benghazi, creating a 9x12 foot hole in the exterior wall. The Omar Abdul Rahman Brigade claimed responsibility for the attack, according to press reporting and a web forum.

- June 8, 2012—Two hand grenades were placed under two parked UK diplomatic vehicles in Sabha (800 km south of Benghazi).

- June 11, 2012—Unknown assailants using two RPGs and small-arms attacked a three-vehicle convoy in Benghazi carrying the British Ambassador.

- June 12, 2012—An RPG attack occurs on the ICRC compound in Misrata (400 km west of Benghazi).
- June 18, 2012—Protestors storm the Tunisian consulate in Benghazi.
- July 29, 2012—An IED is found on grounds of the Tibesti Hotel in Benghazi.
- July 30, 2012—A Sudanese consul in Benghazi is carjacked and his driver is beaten.
- July 31, 2012—Seven Iranian-citizen ICRC workers are abducted in Benghazi.
- August 5, 2012—ICRC Misrata office is attacked with RPGs; ICRC withdraws its representatives from Misrata and Benghazi.
- August 9, 2012—A Spanish-American dual national NGO worker is abducted from the Islamic Cultural Center in Benghazi and released the same day.
- August 20, 2012—A small bomb is thrown at an Egyptian diplomat's vehicle parked outside of the Egyptian consulate in Benghazi.

[52] CIA, "Libya: Struggling To Create Effective Domestic Security System," WIRe, August 29, 2012.
[53] CIA, "Libya: Attack on British Diplomatic Convoy Underscores Risks To Western Interests," WIRe, June 11, 2012.
[54] CIA, "Libya: Recent Attacks Highlight Persistent Threats in Eastern Libya," WIRe, August 1, 2012.
[55] DIA, "Libya: Terrorists Now Targeting U.S. and Western Interests," Defense Intelligence Report, June 12, 2012.
[56] An unknown group fighting under the name of Omar Abdul Rahman, who is commonly referred to as the "Blind Sheikh." The Omar Abdul Rahman Brigade is also referred to as the Omar Abdurrahman group in this report.

- June 12, 2012—The ICRC building in Misratah[57] was attacked by either an RPG or bomb.

- July 17, 2012—Unknown assailants attacked with small arms a three-vehicle, armored UN convoy as it left Darnah (250 km east of Benghazi).

- July 29, 2012—A number of IEDs are found and defused at the Tibesti Hotel in Benghazi. The Tibesti Hotel is frequented by foreign diplomats and businessmen and was previously used by Ambassador Stevens as a base of operations.

- August 1, 2012—The former regime military intelligence building in Benghazi was bombed.

- August 5, 2012—Unknown assailants attacked the ICRC building in Misratah. ICRC facilities in Misratah and Benghazi were attacked four times between May and August, usually with RPGs.[58]

- August 6, 2012—Two U.S. military personnel in diplomatic vehicles were forced off the road and attacked near Tripoli.

In the months prior to the attack, Ambassador Stevens and other State Department officials in Libya outlined concerns via cables to State Department headquarters about the security of the Mission compound in Benghazi and made several requests for additional security resources. For example:

- On June 6, 2012, Stevens recommended the creation of ███████████ ███████ teams, made up of locally hired personnel, in Benghazi and Tripoli.[59] The State Department attempted to create a team in Tripoli, but was unable to do so because it was difficult to find and clear appropriate personnel. A ████████████████ team was never created in Benghazi, despite the Ambassador's recommendation.[60]

---

[57] The IC spells the city "Misratah," but the ARB's report spells it "Misrata."
[58] The IC has since updated this information and now assesses that the ICRC facilities in Misratah and Benghazi were attacked five times between May and August, and on two occasions, the perpetrators used RPGs.
[59] State 12 TRIPOLI 37, June 6, 2012.
[60] SSCI Memorandum for the Record, "Staff Briefing with Under Secretary of State for Management Patrick Kennedy and Assistant Secretary of State for Diplomatic Security Eric Boswell," December 3, 2012.

- On July 9, 2012, Stevens sent a cable to State Department headquarters requesting a minimum of 13 "Temporary Duty" (TDY) U.S. security personnel for Libya, which he said could be made up of DS agents, DoD Site Security Team (SST) personnel, or some combination of the two.[61] These TDY security personnel were needed to meet the requested security posture in Tripoli and Benghazi. The State Department never fulfilled this request and, according to Eric Nordstrom, State Department headquarters never responded to the request with a cable.[62]

- In an August 16, 2012, cable to State headquarters, Stevens raised additional concerns about the deteriorating security situation in Benghazi following an Emergency Action Committee (EAC) meeting held on August 15, 2012, in Benghazi. The EAC is an interagency group convened periodically in U.S. embassies and other facilities in response to emergencies or security matters. In this case, the head State Department officer in Benghazi, called the Principal Officer, convened the meeting "to evaluate Post's tripwires in light of the deteriorating security situation in Benghazi."[63] The cable summarizing this EAC included the following points:

  (1) The Principal Officer "remarked that the security situation in Benghazi was 'trending negatively'" and "that this daily pattern of violence would be the 'new normal' for the foreseeable future, particularly given the minimal capabilities of organizations such as the Supreme Security Council and local police."

  (2) A CIA officer "briefed the EAC on the location of approximately ten Islamist militias and AQ training camps within Benghazi."

  (3) The Principal Officer and a CIA officer "expressed concerns with the lack of host nation security to support the U.S. Mission [facility]."

---

[61] State 12 TRIPOLI 690, July 9, 2012.
[62] SSCI Transcript, *Member and Staff Interview of Eric Nordstrom*, June 27, 2013, pp. 32 and 60.
[63] State 12 TRIPOLI 55, August 16, 2012.

(4) A CIA officer "expressed concerns with Post's relationship with the ██████████████ [local militia], particularly in light of some of the actions taken by the brigade's subsidiary members."

(5) The Regional Security Officer "expressed concerns with the ability to defend Post in the event of a coordinated attack due to limited manpower, security measures, weapons capabilities, host nation support, and the overall size of the compound."

Despite the clearly deteriorating security situation in Benghazi and requests for additional security resources, few significant improvements were made by the State Department to the security posture of the Temporary Mission Facility. Although the Mission facility met the minimum personnel requirements for Diplomatic Security agents as accepted by the U.S. Embassy in Tripoli at the time of the August 15 EAC meeting (specifically, the three Diplomatic Security agents were assigned to guard the Mission compound), the Committee found no evidence that significant actions were taken by the State Department between August 15, 2012, and September 11, 2012, to increase security at the Mission facility in response to the concerns raised in that meeting.[65]

According to the report of the ARB, "there appeared to be very real confusion over who, ultimately, was responsible and empowered to make decisions based on both policy and security concerns" at the State Department's Bureau of Diplomatic Security, Bureau of Near Eastern Affairs, the U.S. Embassy in Tripoli, and the Mission facility in Benghazi.[66] The Independent Panel on Best Practices, which the ARB recommended State establish to identify best practices from other

---

[64] State 12 TRIPOLI 55, August 16, 2012.
[65] The Committee recognizes that there were communications between State Department employees in Libya regarding security during this time period, including an August 22, 2012, document entitled, "Security Requests for U.S. Mission Benghazi" that was sent from DS agents in Benghazi to the RSO in Tripoli that included specific requests for (1) physical security, (2) equipment, and (3) manpower. There is no indication those requests were passed on to State Department Headquarters in the form of a cable.
[66] Unclassified Report of the ARB, December 18, 2012, p. 30.

agencies and countries, found that a "potential root cause for the confusion, lack of clear lines of authority, and communication at the headquarters level" was that "some senior Foreign Service officers and DS agents who met with the Panel identified the Under Secretary for Management (M) as the senior security official in the Department responsible for final decision making regarding critical security requirements," even though this role was "not identified by Congress in the Diplomatic Security Act of 1986."[67]

Additionally, the uncertain future of the Mission facility, due to its one-year expiration in December 2012, contributed to a lack of continuity for security staff and constrained decision-makers in Washington regarding the allocation of security enhancements to that facility.[68] The Temporary Mission Facility continued to be understaffed and under-resourced, a situation best summarized in a June 2012 document from the Principal Officer in Benghazi, commenting that "[i]f there is a real mission, fund us and find the staff."[69] The State Department did implement some physical security improvements in 2012, such as heightening the perimeter wall, installing concrete Jersey barriers, mounting safety grills on the safe area windows, and other minor improvements. However, as the classified version of the ARB report found, the Mission compound "included a weak and very extended perimeter, an incomplete interior fence, no mantraps and unhardened entry gates and doors. Benghazi was also severely under-resourced with regard to weapons, ammunition, [non-lethal deterrents] and fire safety equipment, including escape masks."[70]

In contrast, the CIA, in response to the same deteriorating security situation and IC threat reporting, consistently upgraded its security posture over the same time period. Specifically, the attack on the British Ambassador's convoy by a rocket-propelled grenade on June 11, 2012, led to a CIA security audit of the Annex. As a result, CIA quickly implemented additional security measures due to the threat of continued attacks against Western personnel in Benghazi. These security upgrades included the following:

---

[67] U.S. Department of State, *Report of the Independent Panel on Best Practices,* August 29, 2013, p. 3.
[68] An August 28, 2012, memo entitled, "Regional Security Officer Turnover" from the outgoing RSO stated: "U.S. Mission Benghazi has an uncertain future; Post is scheduled to close December 31, 2012. Various alternatives are being proposed, including colocating with the Annex. The RSO should be aware that requests for expensive security upgrades may be difficult to obtain as headquarters is hesitant to allocate money to a post that may be closing in a few months." Classified Report of the ARB, December 18, 2012, Appendix 6, p. 1.
[69] Email from ███████, "Response from Charlene," February 13, 2012, p. 3 (the document attached to this email is a series of bullet points).
[70] Classified Report of the ARB, December 18, 2012, p. 6.

In addition to these improvements, the physical security of the Annex was much more robust than that of the Mission facility,

[71] CIA BENGHAZI 14986, June 12, 2012, pp. 3 and 5.

[black redaction box]

,"[72] By comparison, as the ARB found, the Mission facility had received additional surveillance cameras, but they remained uninstalled because the State Department had not yet sent out the technical team necessary to install them. In addition, according to the ARB, the camera monitor in the local guard force booth next to the main gate was inoperable on the day of the attacks due to a needed repair by a technical team.[73]

There was also a significant difference in security staffing between the two facilities. In September 2012, there were three Diplomatic Security agents assigned to the Temporary Mission Facility, while there were nine security officers out of a total of █ individuals at the CIA Annex.[74] On the night of the attack, there were five DS agents present at the Mission compound, two of whom came from Tripoli with the Ambassador.[75] In sum, the Mission facility had a much weaker security posture than the Annex, with a significant disparity in the quality and quantity of equipment and security upgrades.

The lack of security enhancements contributed to the security breakdown at the Temporary Mission Facility the night of the attacks. Although the cable following the August 15 Emergency Action Committee stated that requests "for additional physical security upgrades and staffing needs" would be submitted separately to the Embassy in Tripoli,[76] the Committee has not seen any evidence that those requests were passed on by the Embassy, including by the Ambassador, to State Department headquarters before the September 11 attacks in Benghazi.

---

[72] SSCI Transcript, *Member and Staff Interview of former Chief of Base*, December 20, 2012, p. 47.
[73] Unclassified Report of the ARB, December 18, 2012, p. 35.
[74] The █ CIA personnel in Benghazi included [black redaction box]

[75] SSCI Transcript, *Staff Briefing From the Intelligence Community on Benghazi*, November 1, 2012, pp. 7-8.
[76] State 12 TRIPOLI 55, August 16, 2012.

There has been considerable public discussion about the DoD's Site Security Team in Tripoli. The SST, which was provided by the DoD at no expense to the Department of State, consisted of 16 special operations personnel detailed to the Chief of Mission in Libya, although its numbers fluctuated slightly due to rotations. SST personnel were based in and spent most of their time in Tripoli, but traveled to Benghazi two or three times in order to: augment the lack of DS agents there, do a security assessment of the Mission Facility in Benghazi, train local guard forces, deliver excess defense equipment, and improve the security of the Temporary Mission Facility. [77] According to testimony to the Committee, SST personnel carried out a variety of duties including: (1) providing security; (2) clearing unexploded ordnance from the site of the U.S. Embassy compound; (3) establishing secure communications; and (4) carrying out medical duties. [78] The SST provided the Ambassador with various security capabilities and, although not located in Benghazi, provided a greater pool of security resources in Libya from which the State Department could draw.

State Department headquarters made the decision not to request an extension of the SST's mission in August 2012, approximately one month prior to the attacks, because State believed that many of the duties of the SST could be accomplished by local security forces, DS agents, or other State Department capabilities. [79] As a result, DoD changed the mission of its DoD personnel in Libya from protection of the U.S. Embassy to ██████████████ training with the Libyan security forces. [80] ███ ██████████████████████.[81] "DOD wanted to change the nature of the SST team as much as State wanted it changed," according to former DCM Hicks. [82]

DoD confirmed to the Committee that Ambassador Stevens declined two specific offers from General Carter Ham, then the head of AFRICOM, to sustain the SST in the weeks before the terrorist attacks. After reading the August 16, 2012, EAC cable, General Ham called Ambassador Stevens and asked if the Embassy needed the SST from the U.S. military, but Stevens told Ham it did not. Shortly thereafter, Stevens traveled to Germany for a previously scheduled meeting

---

[77] SSCI Transcript, *Benghazi Follow Up with Staff,* May 22, 2013, p. 51.
[78] Ibid., pp. 40-41 and 43-44.
[79] SSCI Transcript, *Hearing on the Attacks in Benghazi,* November 15, 2012, p. 145.
[80] SSCI Transcript, *Member and Staff Interview of Gregory Hicks and Mark Thompson,* June 12, 2013, p. 5.
[81] SSCI Transcript, *Benghazi Follow Up with Staff,* May 22, 2013, p. 42.
[82] SSCI Transcript, *Member and Staff Interview of Gregory Hicks and Mark Thompson,* June 12, 2013, p. 49.

with Ham at AFRICOM headquarters. Ham again offered to sustain the SST at the meeting, and Stevens again declined.[83]

RECOMMENDATION: The State Department must ensure that security threats are quickly assessed and security upgrades are put into place with minimal bureaucratic delay. The State Department has made changes since September 11, 2012, including the creation of a new position of Deputy Assistant Secretary for High-Threat Posts. Although this new position will help the State Department focus on high-threat posts, the State Department must make the institutional changes necessary to quickly and efficiently respond to emerging security threats—especially those threats that have been identified numerous times by the U.S. Intelligence Community. The Committee urges the State Department to consider the recommendation of its Independent Panel on Best Practices to, "as a matter of urgency, establish an Under Secretary for Diplomatic Security" to "bring security governance into the 21st Century and align security management with the realities of a post 9/11 threat environment."[84] As noted by the Chairman of the Independent Panel on Best Practices in his written testimony to a House Committee, this structural recommendation is not new and was suggested in a report written 14 years ago, following the 1998 East Africa Embassy bombings.[85]

RECOMMENDATION: Only in rare instances—and only after a formal risk management plan[86] has been put into place—should State Department facilities that fall short of current security standards[87] be allowed to operate. Facilities that do not meet these standards should be prioritized for additional

---

[83] SSCI Transcript, *Benghazi Follow Up with Staff,* May 22, 2013, p. 47.

[84] U.S. Department of State, *Report of the Independent Panel on Best Practices,* August 29, 2013, pp. 5-6.

[85] Mark Sullivan, Chairman of the Independent Panel on Best Practices, *Testimony Before the House Committee on Oversight and Government Reform,* September 19, 2013, p. 4; *See also* Booz-Allen & Hamilton, *Security and Intelligence Management Study,* October 1999.

[86] As described by the Independent Panel on Best Practices, risk management is balancing the "criticality of the program against the risk to the organization should it implement the program" and understanding, however, there may be "a requirement to conduct critical programs in an environment where the residual risk is so severe that there is a high likelihood its implementation will result in death or serious injury," U.S. Department of State, *Report of the Independent Panel on Best Practices,* August 29, 2013, p. 10.

[87] The "security standards" are required by the Overseas Security Policy Board (OSPB) and the Secure Embassy Construction and Counterterrorism Act of 1999 (SECCA).

security measures.[88] In these cases, temporary facilities should have the physical security, personnel, weapons, ammunition, and fire safety equipment needed to adequately address the threat. The Committee understands the need for State to have the flexibility to operate, on a temporary basis, out of facilities that fall short of these standards; however, these operations are extremely vulnerable, as seen in Benghazi.[89]

RECOMMENDATION: As appropriate, the Deputy Assistant Secretary for High-Threat Posts should also find consistent ways to coordinate with the CIA to exchange best practices for high-threat posts and to discuss common security concerns.

RECOMMENDATION: The IC and State Department should ensure all surveillance cameras at high-risk, high-threat facilities have sufficient resolution, nighttime visibility, remote monitoring capabilities, and redundancy to provide warning and situational awareness in the event of an attack. The Committee notes that the Independent Panel on Best Practices has recommended that the State Department establish a new office "for field expedient deployment of hardware, cutting-edge protective technology and procedures."[90]

FINDING #3: There was no singular "tactical warning" in the intelligence reporting leading up to the events on September 11, 2012, predicting an attack on U.S. facilities in Benghazi on the 9/11 anniversary, although State and the

---

[88] The State Department's Office of Inspector General has recommended that components within the Department "develop minimum security standards that must be met prior to occupying facilities located in the Department of State-designated high-risk, high-threat environments and include new minimum security standards of occupancy in the *Foreign Affairs Handbook* as appropriate." U.S. Department of State, Office of Inspector General (IG), *Special Review of the Accountability Review Board Process,* September 2013, p. 29.

[89] The Independent Panel on Best Practices said: "Waivers for not meeting security standards have become common place in the [State] Department; however, without a risk management process to identify and implement alternate mitigating measures after a waiver has been given, Department employees, particularly those in high threat areas, could be exposed to an unacceptable level of risk." U.S. Department of State, *Report of the Independent Panel on Best Practices,* August 29, 2013, p. 8. A recent State IG report also found: "The Department of State has neither a conceptual framework nor a process for risk management. There is no one person or office specifically tasked to oversee the assessment of risks in critical, high-threat locales and weigh those risks against the U.S. Government's policy priorities to determine if the strategic value of the program outweighs the associated risk." U.S. Department of State, Office of the Inspector General, *Special Review of the Accountability Review Board Process,* September 2013, p. 1.

[90] U.S. Department of State, *Report of the Independent Panel on Best Practices,* August 29, 2013, p. 23.

CIA both sent general warning notices to facilities worldwide noting the potential security concerns associated with the anniversary. Such a specific warning should not have been expected, however, given the limited intelligence collection of the Benghazi area at the time.

To date, the Committee has not identified any intelligence or other information received prior to September 11, 2012, by the IC or State Department indicating specific terrorist planning to attack the U.S. facilities in Benghazi on September 11, 2012.

Although it did not reach the U.S. Intelligence Community until after the attacks, it is important to note that a former Transitional National Council (TNC) security official in Benghazi, ███████, had received information of a possible imminent attack against the Mission facility in advance. The official said that approximately four hours prior to the attack, he attempted to notify the Libyan Intelligence Service (LIS) that an attack was expected, but he was unable to reach two contacts he had in the LIS as they were out of the country.[91] The CIA has been unable to corroborate the official's claim that he attempted to provide the LIS with advance warning about the attack.

[92]

---

[91] NCTC and FBI, *The 11-12 September Attacks on US Facilities in Benghazi,* November 13, 2012, p. 3.
[92] Email from CIA Office of Congressional Affairs staff to SSCI Staff, "Answers to SSCI Benghazi Questions from August 2013," September 6, 2013.

According to a January 4, 2013, letter from the Acting Director of the CIA, Michael Morell, "[t]he nature of the attacks suggested they did not involve significant pre-planning."[96] Although it may never be known with complete certainty, it is possible that the individuals and groups involved in the attacks had not planned on conducting those attacks until that day, meaning that specific tactical warning would have been highly unlikely. However, intelligence reports made clear that extremist groups in eastern Libya, including Ansar al-Sharia, were not only running training camps there, but also plotting and carrying out attacks against U.S. and Western interests in the months prior to the attacks in Benghazi.

---

[93] SSCI Transcript, *Briefing from the Intelligence Community on Benghazi,* November 1, 2012, p. 59-62; SSCI Transcript, *Benghazi Follow Up with Staff,* May 22, 2013, pp. 67-69.
[94] Email from NSA staff ████████ to ████████, et al, September 12, 2012, 05:37 a.m.
[95] Email from CIA staff ████████ to "████" (staff of the CIA Directorate of Intelligence), September 16, 2012, 08:44 a.m.
[96] Letter from Acting CIA Director Michael Morell to SSCI Chairman Dianne Feinstein, January 4, 2013.

.”[97]   However, the collective assessment of the IC remains that the attacks "were deliberate and organized, but that their lethality and efficacy did not necessarily indicate extensive planning."[98]

RECOMMENDATION: The IC must place a greater emphasis on collecting intelligence and open-source information, including extremist-affiliated social media, to improve its ability to provide tactical warnings, especially in North Africa, the Middle East, and other areas where the U.S. has facilities under high threat. Given the current resource-constrained budget environment, the Committee is working with the IC to identify resource gaps and realign assets to focus on those gaps, especially in North Africa.

FINDING #4: Although the IC relied heavily on open source press reports in the immediate aftermath of the attacks, the IC conducted little analysis of open source extremist-affiliated social media prior to and immediately after the attacks.

Although it is impossible to draw definitive conclusions, there were fragmentary reports from the IC indicating that more in-depth intelligence exploitation of social media in the Benghazi area, including web postings by Libyan nationals employed at the Temporary Mission Facility, could have flagged potential security threats to the Mission facility or important information about the employees prior to the September 11, 2012, attacks.

RECOMMENDATION: The IC should expand its capabilities to conduct analysis of open source information including extremist-affiliated social media particularly in areas where it is hard to develop human intelligence or there has been recent political upheaval. Analysis of extremist-affiliated social media should be more clearly integrated into analytic products, when appropriate.

---

[97] CIA, "Libya: Update on Planning and Culpability for Benghazi Attacks," WIRe, March 29, 2013.
[98] Ibid; SSCI Transcript, *Benghazi Follow Up with Staff*, May 22, 2013, p. 6.

FINDING #5: There were "tripwires" designed to prompt a reduction in personnel or the suspension of operations at the Mission facility in Benghazi and although there is evidence that some of them had been crossed, operations continued with minimal change. Some nations closed their diplomatic facilities in Benghazi as the security conditions deteriorated during the summer of 2012, but other nations stayed along with the United States, contrary to some public reports and statements that the U.S. was the last country represented in Benghazi.

State Department documents indicate that its Bureau of Near Eastern Affairs was aware of the fact that many of the tripwires had indeed been crossed and discussed suspending operations, but never did. Given these developments and the available intelligence at the time, the Committee believes the State Department should have recognized the need to increase security to a level commensurate with the threat, or suspend operations in Benghazi. However, operations continued with minimal improvements in security and personnel protections. Although some countries and international organizations had reduced their presence in Benghazi, the United States maintained a diplomatic presence there similar to the UN, the European Union, and other Western countries such as Italy, France, Turkey, and Malta.[99]

There were plans to co-locate the Mission facility and the Annex starting in 2013, but no changes were made before the September 11, 2012, attacks. The Chief of Base stated that there had been discussions with Ambassador Stevens about co-locating the Annex and the State Department compound at the same facility. "We had been actively looking," he said. "We had had our officers come out there to survey different locations in Benghazi to look for a location that we could co-locate with the State Department, and we were planning to do that before the end of this [2012] calendar year. So there was absolutely a plan to do that."[100]

RECOMMENDATION: Where adequate security is not available, the Department of State should be prepared to evacuate or close diplomatic facilities under the highest threat, as it has in recent years in Sana'a, Yemen, and Damascus, Syria.

---

[99] Email from U.S. Department of State, Office of Legislative Affairs to SSCI staff, December 6, 2013, 5:00 p.m.
[100] SSCI Transcript, *Member and Staff Interview of former Chief of Base*, December 20, 2012, p. 7.

> **RECOMMENDATION:** The Committee supports the recommendations of the Accountability Review Board to bring greater collaboration and connectivity between the State Department's Bureau of Diplomatic Security and the Intelligence Community.[101] The Department of State must pay special attention to the "on the ground" assessments of IC and State personnel in the field and IC analytic products about assessed risks to specific U.S. facilities overseas.

Response During the Attacks

> **FINDING #6:** The State Department personnel at the Temporary Mission Facility in Benghazi relied on the security officers at the CIA Annex as a last resort for security in the event of an attack.

Although there was no formal written agreement about how security should be handled between the two facilities in Benghazi, there was a common understanding that each group would come to the other's aid if attacked, which is what happened the night of September 11, 2012.[102] IC personnel immediately came to the aid of their colleagues at the Temporary Mission Facility, and fought bravely to secure TMF personnel and their own Annex facility. The Committee interviewed U.S. personnel in Benghazi that night, and they credited their lives being saved to the personnel who responded to the attacks.

With respect to the role of DoD and AFRICOM in emergency evacuations and rescue operations in Benghazi, the Committee received conflicting information on the extent of the awareness within DoD of the Benghazi Annex. According to U.S. AFRICOM, neither the command nor its Commander were aware of an annex

---

[101] The Committee also supports the "positive changes" noted by the Independent Panel on Best Practices that are "currently underway or planned within DS, with Department support, for both better intelligence access and additional intelligence analyst positions. Specifically, liaison representatives from the National Counterterrorism Center (NCTC), the National Geospatial[-Intelligence] Agency (NGA), and the National Security Agency (NSA) have been assigned to DS/ITA [Diplomatic Security/Intelligence and Threat Analysis] .... Additionally, nine positions for overseas deployed Intelligence Research Analysts have been approved for Fiscal Year (FY) 2014." U.S. Department of State, *Report of the Independent Panel on Best Practices,* August 29, 2013, p. 18.
[102] SSCI Transcript, *Member and Staff Interview of former Chief of Base*, December 20, 2012, p. 6. The Chief of Base said: "We had a 100 percent unwritten plan to go to their aid in the case of an emergency. But there was nothing written."

in Benghazi, Libya.[103] However, it is the Committee's understanding that other DoD personnel were aware of the Benghazi Annex.

> **RECOMMENDATION**: There should be more specific information exchanged between DoD and the IC, through the appropriate channels, to make regional Combatant Commanders aware of the general presence of Intelligence Community personnel in their areas of responsibility for the purposes of emergency evacuations and rescue. This information could have been helpful to the Commander of AFRICOM and should have been more easily available to him.

> **FINDING #7**: There were no U.S. military resources in position to intervene in short order in Benghazi to help defend the Temporary Mission Facility and its Annex on September 11 and 12, 2012.

DoD moved aerial assets, teams of Marines, and special operations forces toward Libya as the attacks were ongoing, but in addition to the seven-man reinforcement team from Tripoli, the only additional resources that were able to arrive on scene were unmanned, unarmed aerial surveillance assets. The unmanned aerial vehicle that flew to Benghazi that night ███████████ ████████████████████████████████████ when he could not be found at the Temporary Mission Facility.[104]

According to Major General Darryl Roberson, Vice Director of Operations for the Joint Staff:

> There were no ships available to provide any support that were anywhere close to the facility at Benghazi. The assets that we had available were Strike Eagles loaded with live weapons that could have responded, but they were located in Djibouti, which is the equivalent of the distance between here [Washington D.C.] and Los Angeles. The other fighters that might have been available were located in Aviano, Italy. They were not loaded with weapons. They were not on an alert status. We would've had to build weapons, load weapons, get tankers to support it, and get it there. There was

---

[103] Email from Office of the Chairman of the Joint Chief of Staff for Legislative Affairs to SSCI staff, August 15, 2013, 5:14 p.m.
[104] SSCI Transcript, *Member and Staff Interview of former Chief of Base*, December 20, 2012, pp. 63-64.

no way that we were going to be able to do that. Unfortunately, there was not a carrier in the Mediterranean that could have been able to support; the assets that we mobilized immediately were the only assets we had available to try to support.[105]

The Committee has reviewed the allegations that U.S. personnel, including in the IC or DoD, prevented the mounting of any military relief effort during the attacks, but the Committee has not found any of these allegations to be substantiated. The following assets were deployed or in the process of deploying in response to the Benghazi attacks (based on a review of DoD documents and testimony before the Committee):

- The six-man CIA security team (plus an interpreter) left from the Annex to respond to the Temporary Mission Facility soon after it came under attack. The CIA security team did not make it in time to save Ambassador Stevens and Sean Smith, but they successfully evacuated the other Americans at the Mission facility to the Annex.

- As noted, one unarmed Predator was diverted to provide surveillance coverage of the Temporary Mission Facility as it was being attacked. This Predator was subsequently replaced by another unarmed Predator to enable the first Predator to return to base for refueling.

- A seven-person security team (consisting of two DoD personnel, four CIA personnel, and a linguist) flew from the U.S. Embassy in Tripoli to Benghazi and successfully helped evacuate the Americans from the Annex to the airport. It is important to clarify that, at the time of the attacks in Benghazi, there were six DoD personnel assigned to Embassy Tripoli. Four employees were under Special Operations Command Africa (SOC-AFRICA) and reported through a similar, but separate, chain of command within AFRICOM. The other two individuals from that team were DoD personnel working ▓▓▓▓▓▓ (based on a memorandum of understanding) under a separate special operations task force. According to the DoD, the four staff under SOC-AFRICA were told by their command to stay to protect Embassy Tripoli due to concerns of a similar attack in Tripoli.[106]

---

[105] SSCI Transcript, *Hearing on the Attacks in Benghazi*, November 15, 2012, pp. 68-69.
[106] SSCI Transcript, *Benghazi Follow Up with Staff*, May 22, 2013, pp. 42-45.

- Sometime between midnight and 2:00 a.m. Benghazi time, Secretary of Defense Leon Panetta verbally ordered two Marine Fleet Antiterrorism Security Teams (or "FAST platoons") to deploy from their base in Rota, Spain, to Libya.

  o One team was to go to Benghazi to respond to the attack on the Temporary Mission Facility.

  o One team was to deploy to Tripoli to protect the Embassy if it was attacked.

  o The first FAST platoon would take ▇ hours to be airborne. As Major General Roberson testified, "whenever they got the notification, ▇ hours later they are supposed to be airborne and moving to wherever they need to."[107] The second FAST platoon would have taken 96 hours to deploy, according to Roberson.[108]

  o Because all Americans were evacuated from Benghazi before the first FAST platoon could arrive, it was diverted to protect the U.S. Embassy in Tripoli and arrived at 8:56 p.m. Tripoli time, on September 12, 2012.[109]

- Sometime between midnight and 2:00 a.m. Benghazi time, Secretary Panetta also ordered two teams of special operations forces to Benghazi, but like the FAST platoons, neither made it to Libya before the Americans had already evacuated the next morning after the attack.

  o One special operations force—which was training in Croatia—was ordered to prepare to deploy to an intermediate NATO staging base in Sigonella, Italy.

  o The other special operations force—based in the United States— was ordered to deploy to the intermediate NATO staging base at Sigonella.

---

[107] SSCI Transcript, *Hearing on the Attacks in Benghazi*, November 15, 2012, p. 146.
[108] Ibid.
[109] DoD, *Timeline of Department of Defense Actions on September 11-12, 2012*, p. 2.

o The first special operations force would take ▮ hours to be airborne. As Major General Roberson testified: "The CIF [Commanders In-Extremis Force] in Croatia is on an ▮▮▮" meaning it would take ▮ hours of preparation time before it could begin the flight from Croatia to Benghazi.[110] The CIF from Croatia only made it to the staging base at Sigonella by 7:57 p.m. Benghazi time, on September 12, almost 10 hours after all Americans were evacuated from Benghazi.[111]

o The other special operations force—from the United States—did not arrive at the staging base at Sigonella until 9:28 p.m. Benghazi time, on September 12.[112]

- There have been congressional and public questions about why military assets were not used from the U.S. military base in Souda Bay, Crete. The Chairman of the Joint Chiefs of Staff, General Martin Dempsey, testified before the Senate Armed Services Committee on February 7, 2013, that (1) the military asset in Souda Bay, Crete, "wasn't the right tool for the particular threat we faced;" (2) "...the aircraft were not among the forces that we had at heightened alert;" and (3) the "boots-on-the-ground capabilities" that DoD deployed would have arrived too late, so they did not deploy to Benghazi.[113]

o Two months after the attacks in Benghazi, DoD moved a FAST platoon from Rota, Spain, to Souda Bay, Crete, reducing its preparation time to ▮▮▮▮.[114]

RECOMMENDATION: It is imperative that the State Department, DoD, and the IC work together to identify and prioritize the largest gaps in coverage for the protection of U.S. diplomatic, military, and intelligence personnel in the North Africa region and other high-threat posts around the world. The small number of U.S. military resources devoted to the vast and

---

[110] SSCI Transcript, *Hearing on the Attacks in Benghazi*, November 15, 2012, p. 146.
[111] DoD, *Timeline of Department of Defense Actions on September 11-12, 2012*, p. 2.
[112] Ibid.
[113] Martin Dempsey, Chairman of the Joint Chiefs of Staff General, *Testimony before the Senate Armed Services Committee during Hearing on the Terrorist Attacks on U.S. Facilities in Benghazi, Libya*, February 7, 2013.
[114] SSCI Transcript, *Hearing on the Attacks in Benghazi*, November 15, 2012, p. 152.

often ungoverned North African landscape makes it unlikely that DoD can respond in short periods to all potential crises across North Africa. If DoD cannot always provide help in an emergency, U.S. personnel on the ground must make alternative plans to evacuate in the event of an attack or if intelligence indicates that an attack is imminent.

FINDING #8: Unarmed U.S. military surveillance assets were not delayed when responding to the attack, and they provided important situational awareness for those under siege during the attacks against the Temporary Mission Facility and the Annex on September 11 and 12, 2012.

At the direction of AFRICOM, at 10 p.m. Benghazi time, DoD moved a remotely piloted, unarmed surveillance aircraft, which was already conducting a separate intelligence mission over Darnah, to airspace above the Mission facility. It arrived at approximately 11:10 p.m. Benghazi time, shortly before the U.S. security personnel evacuated to the Annex. A second remotely piloted, unarmed surveillance aircraft relieved the first, and monitored the eventual evacuation of personnel from the Annex to the Benghazi airport later on the morning of September 12, 2012. According to a CIA cable which served as the joint report from Tripoli Station and Benghazi Base on the attacks: "ISR coverage was [a] crucial resource ███████████████ .... ISR was also crucial to provide situational awareness to Benghazi Base and Team Tripoli efforts on the ground."[115]

The Intelligence Picture After the Attacks

FINDING #9: In finished reports after September 11, 2012, intelligence analysts inaccurately referred to the presence of a protest at the Mission facility before the attack based on open source information and limited intelligence, but without sufficient intelligence or eyewitness statements to corroborate that assertion. The IC took too long to correct these erroneous reports, which caused confusion and influenced the public statements of policymakers.

---

[115] CIA TRIPOLI 27900, September 19, 2012, p. 9.

In the immediate aftermath of the attacks, the IC received numerous reports, both classified and unclassified, which provided contradictory accounts that there were demonstrations at the Temporary Mission Facility. In some cases, these intelligence reports—which were disseminated widely in the Intelligence Community—contained references to press reports on protests that were simply copied into intelligence products. Other reporting indicated there were no protests. For example, the IC obtained closed circuit television video from the Mission facility ████████████████████████, and there were credible eyewitness statements of U.S. personnel on the ground that night, which the FBI began to collect from interviewing survivors starting on September 15, 2012, in Ramstein Air Base, Germany.

The IC also had information that there were no protests outside the Temporary Mission Facility prior to the attacks, but did not incorporate that information into its widely circulated assessments in a timely manner. Contrary to many press reports at the time, eyewitness statements by U.S. personnel indicate that there were no protests at the start of the attacks. For example, on September 15, 2012, the CIA's Chief of Station in Tripoli sent to the then-Deputy Director of the CIA and others at the CIA an email that reported the attacks were "not/not an escalation of protests."[116] Yet, the CIA's January 4, 2013, Analytic Line Review downplays the importance of this email, noting, ". . . as a standard practice, we do not base analysis on e-mails and other informal communications from the field because such accounts often change when formalized as disseminated intelligence reports."[117]

Moreover, it appears this reporting from those present during the attacks did not make its way into assessments at CIA Headquarters, as the Deputy Director of the Middle East and North Africa Analysis Office at CIA wrote an internal email, dated September 16, 2012, that mentioned "protestors that preceded the violence."[118] On September 18, 2012, the FBI and CIA reviewed the closed circuit television video from the Mission facility that showed there were no protests prior to the attacks. Although information gathered from interviews with U.S. personnel who were on the ground during the attacks was shared informally between the FBI

---

[116] CIA, *Analytical Line Review of the Benghazi Attacks*, January 4, 2013, p. 7.
[117] Ibid., p. 8.
[118] Email from ████████████ to ████████, "FW: DCIA/DDCIA Memo as sent to DD/DI ████████," September 16, 2012, 4:08 p.m., p. 1.

and CIA, it was not until two days later, on September 20, 2012, that the FBI disseminated its intelligence reports detailing such interviews.[119]

A dearth of clear and definitive HUMINT or eyewitness reporting led IC analysts to rely on open press reports and limited SIGINT reporting that incorrectly attributed the origins of the Benghazi attacks to "protests," over first-hand accounts from U.S. officials on the ground. CIA's January 4, 2013, Analytic Line Review found that "[a]pproximately a dozen reports that included press accounts, public statements by AAS members, HUMINT reporting, DOD reporting, and signals intelligence all stated or strongly suggested that a protest occurred outside of the Mission facility just prior to the attacks."[120]

Of the 11 reports cited by the CIA's Analytic Line Review, six were press articles, two were the public statements of Ansar al-Sharia, and the three others were intelligence reports. Specific open source reports and intelligence on which analysts appear to have based their judgments include the public statements by Ansar al-Sharia that the attacks were a "spontaneous and popular uprising."[121] Also, there was protest activity in Egypt and approximately 40 other cities around the world and violent attacks against U.S. diplomatic facilities in Tunisia, Yemen, and Egypt from September 11-20, 2012. In addition, there were intelligence reports in the days following the Benghazi attacks that al-Qa'ida-associated terrorists hoped to take advantage of global protests for further attacks.[122]

As a result of evidence from closed circuit videos and other reports, the IC changed its assessment about a protest in classified intelligence reports on September 24, 2012, to state there were no demonstrations or protests at the Temporary Mission Facility prior to the attacks. This slow change in the official assessment affected the public statements of government officials, who continued to state in press interviews that there were protests outside the Mission compound. The IC continues to assess that although they do not think the first attack came out of protests, the lethality and efficacy of the attack "did not require significant

[119] ODNI, *Intelligence Community Response: Fact-Based & Substantive Review Only Regarding SSCI Report of Terrorist Attacks on U.S. Facilities in Benghazi,* August 30, 2013, p. 15.
[120] CIA, *Analytical Line Review of the Benghazi Attacks,* January 4, 2013, p. 4.
[121] ODNI, *The Benghazi Intelligence Review,* October 22, 2012, translated transcript of an open source YouTube video: "Libya: Ansar Al-Shari'ah Video Statement on US Consulate Attack in Benghazi," September 12, 2012, p. 2.
[122] NCTC, "Libya: Variety of Extremists Participated in Benghazi Attacks," NCTC Current, September 15, 2012.

amounts of preplanning."[123] The IC continues to review the amount and nature of any preplanning that went into the attacks.[124]

RECOMMENDATION: Intelligence analysts should more aggressively request and integrate eyewitness reporting—especially from U.S. Government personnel—in the aftermath of a crisis. The IC should establish a process or reevaluate its current procedures to improve the speed and process with which operational reporting (for example, eyewitness reporting) and raw collection make it into disseminated intelligence products.

RECOMMENDATION: The IC must act quickly to correct the written record and address misperceptions in its finished analytical products. The IC should avoid repeating erroneous information in its intelligence products as analysts continued to do when they wrote there were "protests" at the Temporary Mission Facility, which then made its way into reports disseminated to U.S. policymakers and Congress.

FINDING #10: The State Department Bureau of Intelligence and Research (INR) did not disseminate any independent analysis in the year following the Benghazi attacks.

Based on the Committee's review, the State Department's INR disseminated no intelligence products related to the Benghazi attacks in the year following the attacks. Considering the attacks began on a State Department facility, involved the deaths of two State Department personnel, and were an important indication of escalating threats against U.S. facilities and personnel in the region, the Committee finds it unsettling that INR chose not to, or was unable to, disseminate any analysis related to the attacks or the implications of the attacks.

INR witnesses told Committee staff that its staff resources were scarce, but also said that "…unless we have something that is unique analysis that is really going to change things we feel that we're better off coordinating on what the IC says then briefing within our building."[125]

---

[123] SSCI Transcript, *Benghazi Follow Up with Staff*, May 22, 2013, p. 82.
[124] Ibid.
[125] SSCI Transcript, *Staff Briefing: U.S. Department of State Bureau of Intelligence and Research Re: Benghazi*, February 1, 2013, p. 47.

Yet, INR officials have access to State Department information and perspectives that many in the Intelligence Community do not; therefore, INR should play a more active—not just a coordinating—role in analysis for the IC and not just the State Department. The State Department's Inspector General went even further and found that INR should be the office to produce a comprehensive security assessment for each post based on all available diplomatic and intelligence sources.[126]

RECOMMENDATION: The Committee urges the DNI and the State Department to conduct a review of the types of intelligence products that INR prepares and to look for ways to make INR's products more timely and responsive to world events, especially those that directly affect State Department personnel. The Committee notes that the Independent Panel on Best Practices has also recommended that the State Department audit and assess "how quickly and effectively INR shares intelligence with DS and all other [State] Department components."[127]

FINDING #11: The DNI's Office of Analytic Integrity and Standards (AIS) failed to provide complete and accurate information to Congress during its review of the Benghazi attacks. The Committee found AIS's methodology in assembling documents to be flawed. Despite repeated requests from the Committee, AIS also refused to provide complete, accurate, and thoroughly cited information to Congress.

In response to inquiries by Members of Congress about the intelligence reporting before, during, and after the Benghazi attacks, the DNI's office stated that all intelligence reports on Benghazi would be assembled by AIS and those hundreds of documents would be provided to the congressional intelligence committees as part of an official "Benghazi Intelligence Review" (BIR).

The BIR documents were delivered on October 22, 2012, but were not a complete set of intelligence reporting related to the Benghazi attacks. The Committee found that there was significant confusion within AIS about their

---

[126] U.S. Department of State, Office of Inspector General, *Special Review of the Accountability Review Board Process,* September 2013, p. 30.
[127] U.S. Department of State, *Report of the Independent Panel on Best Practices,* August 29, 2013, p. 20.

efforts to bring together documents for the BIR. Although the review was presented to the Committee as comprehensive, it was not even thorough. The Committee found that AIS believed it was tasked to find some illustrative documents (that may not have been verified by analysts as significant or priority documents), as opposed to providing all Benghazi documents to Congress. The Committee is concerned that AIS, the office within the Intelligence Community charged with setting and evaluating the standards for analysis, could perform so poorly in responding to a request from the Committee.

The Talking Points

On September 15, 2012, the CIA provided to the House and Senate Intelligence Committees a set of unclassified talking points at the request of the House Permanent Select Committee on Intelligence. The talking points and the emails, in redacted form, detailing their coordination are now available to the public and the Committee encourages the public to review them. Members of the Committee have differing views on the substance of, and circumstances surrounding, the CIA's talking points that are addressed in the Additional Views of this report. A detailed timeline of the different versions of the talking points is in Appendix I of this report.

> **RECOMMENDATION**: **In responding to future requests for unclassified talking points from Congress, the Intelligence Community should simply tell Congress which facts are unclassified and let Members of Congress provide additional context for the public.**

Lessons Learned After the Attacks to Improve the Interaction between the State Department's Bureau of Diplomatic Security and the IC

The Benghazi attacks demonstrate that U.S. facilities are at risk of being attacked at any time, without specific tactical warning; therefore, security at all high-risk overseas U.S. Government facilities must be improved and reevaluated on an ongoing basis as threats change and emerge. The IC is playing a key role in that review process by helping to evaluate the threats and strengthen the security of its own facilities. The State Department and the IC should share best practices whenever possible to improve security to high-risk, high-threat posts. As noted, additional security measures were implemented in a timely manner by the CIA at the Annex, yet not at the Temporary Mission Facility.

The Department of State has missed opportunities to draw lessons from past events that could improve security programs and enhance security for the entire foreign affairs community, according to the September 2013 "Special Review of the Accountability Review Board Process," by the State Department's Inspector General.[128]

FINDING #12: The co-location of IC and diplomatic personnel in Benghazi could have enhanced security; but co-location often presents tradeoffs that should be carefully evaluated in high-threat environments.

Keeping intelligence facilities separate from State Department compounds can provide important operational advantages. According to the Chief of Base: "We had the luxury that the Mission didn't have of keeping our compound very low-profile and making our movements—we used very good ████████████ protocol movements, and our vehicular moves were very much low-profile. So we had a security advantage, I guess you could say, over our State colleagues." A June 12, 2012, CIA cable from Benghazi Base came to a similar conclusion, finding: "…as a direct result of a concerted effort to build and maintain a low profile we believe that the locals for the most part do not know we are here and housed/officed in a separate stand alone facility from our [United States Government] USG counterparts."[129]

RECOMMENDATION: The Committee agrees that IC and diplomatic personnel should generally be co-located overseas except where the IC determines that, for operational reasons, co-location is not helpful in meeting mission objectives or that it poses a security risk. In those limited instances, the IC should work with the State Department in light of Chief of Mission authorities. However, the Committee does not believe that co-location decisions should be subjected to a broader interagency approval process.

---

[128] U.S. Department of State, Office of the Inspector General, *Special Review of the Accountability Review Board Process,* September 2013, p. 1; *see also* U.S. Department of State, Office of Inspector General, *Audit of Department of State Compliance With Physical and Procedural Security Standards at Selected High Threat Level Posts,* June 2013.
[129] CIA BENGHAZI 14986, June 12, 2012, p. 2.

> **FINDING #13:** The primary source of security for the Temporary Mission Facility, local Libyan militia members, failed to provide any significant defense of the compound from the attack.

Video footage shows—and the ARB also found—that, at 9:42 p.m. Benghazi time, a local police vehicle stationed outside the Mission facility withdrew as soon as armed attackers advanced toward the U.S. compound. In addition, the TMF in Benghazi had been vandalized and attacked in the months prior to the September 11-12 attacks by some of the same guards who were there to protect it.[130]

Local security guards, especially security guards who are not operated and overseen by the host government, are an inherently less reliable security force than security provided by U.S. forces or the military or police forces of a host government. According to the State Department, the Mission facility did not store classified information, and therefore no Marine contingent was present.[131] Although U.S. Government security forces are always preferred, the CIA and State determined that local militias would provide the so-called "least bad option" in post-revolutionary Libya. The former Chief of Base stated: "There was no alternative. You know, there really is no functioning government there. And the militia groups that both we, and the State Department, depended on were in fact kind of the de facto government there in Benghazi."[132]

The Government of Libya lacked the capacity to respond to the crisis militarily or with law enforcement personnel. Its governance over the entire Benghazi area was also extremely limited, which further constrained its ability to respond. The ineffectiveness of the Libyan government in its ability to respond to emergencies and control areas like Benghazi was well-known to the U.S. Government and Ambassador Stevens prior to the attacks. In fact, on August 29, 2012, the CIA published an intelligence report entitled, "Libya: Struggling to

---

[130] Classified Report of the ARB, December 18, 2012, Appendix 26.
[131] Also, according to the official website of the U.S. Marine Corps: "The primary mission of the Marine Security Guard (MSG) is to provide internal security at designated U.S. diplomatic and consular facilities in order to prevent the compromise of classified material vital to the national security of the United States." *See* www.mcesg.marines.mil, accessed December 5, 2013.
[132] SSCI Transcript, *Member and Staff Interview of former Chief of Base*, December 20, 2012, p. 20.

Create Effective Domestic Security System" that highlighted the Libyan Government's inability to prevent or respond to security incidents.[133]

RECOMMENDATION: The U.S. Government cannot rely on local security in areas where the U.S. has facilities under high-threat or where the host nation is not capable of providing adequate security. The Committee supports the State Department's initiative—working with DoD—to request additional Marines and to expand the Marine Security Guard Program to increase protection at high-risk facilities beyond solely the protection of classified information.

RECOMMENDATION: Based on the fact that Ambassador Stevens and Sean Smith perished due to the smoke from fires lit by attackers, State and the IC should review the fire safety and high-threat training and equipment for all employees sent abroad to ensure that proper fire safety equipment is available at all facilities and personnel have proper protective equipment in the event of smoke and fire emergencies.

Bringing the Attackers to Justice

FINDING #14: More than a year after the Benghazi attacks, the terrorists who perpetrated the attacks have still not been brought to justice. The IC has identified several individuals responsible for the attacks. Some of the individuals have been identified with a strong level of confidence. However, insight into the current whereabouts and links between these individuals in some cases is limited due in part to the nascent intelligence capabilities in the region.

Individuals affiliated with terrorist groups, including AQIM, Ansar al-Sharia,[134] AQAP, and the Mohammad Jamal Network, participated in the September 11, 2012, attacks. Intelligence suggests that the attack was not a highly coordinated plot, but was opportunistic; however, well-armed attackers easily overwhelmed the Libyan security guards and the five U.S. Diplomatic Security agents present at the Temporary Mission Facility. It remains unclear if any group

---

[133] CIA, "Libya: Struggling To Create Effective Domestic Security System," WIRe, August 29, 2012.

[134] After the Benghazi attacks, the IC began to distinguish Ansar al-Sharia into two groups: (1) AAS-Benghazi; and (2) AAS-Darnah.

or person exercised overall command and control of the attacks or whether extremist group leaders directed their members to participate. Some intelligence suggests the attacks were likely put together in short order, following that day's violent protests in Cairo against an inflammatory video, suggesting that these and other terrorist groups could conduct similar attacks with little advance warning.

The FBI's investigation into the individuals responsible for the Benghazi attacks has been hampered by inadequate cooperation and a lack of capacity by foreign governments to hold these perpetrators accountable, making the pursuit of justice for the attacks slow and insufficient. As a result, key information gaps remain about the potential foreknowledge and complicity of Libyan militia groups and security forces, the level of pre-planning for the attacks, the perpetrators and their involvement in other terrorist activites, and the motivation for the attacks.

The Libyan Government has not shown the political incentive or will within its own country to seek out, arrest, and prosecute individuals believed to be associated with the attacks. Furthermore, the security environment in Benghazi remains extremely dangerous for individuals wishing to work with the U.S. Government on its investigation into the attacks. In testimony before the Senate Appropriations Subcommittee on Commerce, Justice, Science, and Related Agencies, then-FBI Director Robert Mueller noted that as many as 15 individuals supporting the investigation or otherwise helpful to the United States have been killed in Benghazi since the attacks, underscoring the lawless and chaotic circumstances in eastern Libya. It is unclear whether their killings were related to the Benghazi investigation.[135]

RECOMMENDATION: The U.S. Government must swiftly bring the attackers to justice, in spite of the unwillingness or lack of capacity of the Libyan government to assist in this effort.

---

[135] Robert S. Mueller III, Director of the FBI, *Testimony before the Senate Appropriations Subcommittee on Commerce, Justice and Science*, May 16, 2013.

V. CONCLUSION

In the year since Chris Stevens, Sean Smith, Tyrone Woods, and Glen Doherty were killed during the terrorist attacks on U.S. facilities in Benghazi, Libya, the Senate Intelligence Committee has worked to understand the events leading up to, during, and after these attacks. Although this report does not attempt to address every aspect of this tragedy, we believe it identifies important findings and recommendations that will improve our intelligence analysis, priorities, and capabilities and help ensure the future safety of U.S. personnel serving overseas.

We recognize, particularly in this post-9/11 era, that the risk to U.S. diplomatic, military, and intelligence officials around the world remains high. We cannot eliminate this risk, but we can and must do more to minimize the potential harm to the men and women who, understanding and accepting this risk, have chosen to serve the United States abroad. Unfortunately, as we learned in Benghazi, the tactical intelligence that can warn of an imminent threat is not always present. This cannot be an excuse for inaction, however. It is imperative that the Intelligence Community position itself to anticipate, rather than just react to, potential terrorism hotspots and changing dynamics on the ground, and that U.S. personnel and facilities overseas are equipped to immediately defend against and withstand any potential attack. It is also imperative that those in decision-making positions in Washington, D.C. heed the concerns and wisdom of those on the front lines and make resource and security decisions with those concerns in mind. The United States government did not meet this standard of care in Benghazi, but we believe this report's findings and recommendations will help avoid similar tragedies.

The Committee honors the lives and sacrifices of the four American heroes who died in Benghazi on September 11, 2012. We also recognize those who came to their aid or mobilized assistance in their defense. This report cannot in any way compensate for the sacrifices of these individuals, but it is our hope that we can, as a nation, resolve to do all that is needed to protect the lives and well-being of every American citizen serving this country abroad.

APPENDIX I: The Benghazi Talking Points

On September 15, 2012, the CIA provided the HPSCI and the SSCI with unclassified talking points for Members' use in media and public statements regarding the September 11, 2012, terrorist attacks in Benghazi, Libya. The talking points were requested by the HPSCI during a meeting with then-CIA Director Petraeus on Friday, September 14, 2012. As made clear by 100 pages of emails released by the Obama Administration on May 15, 2013,[136] the talking points were then also provided to U.S. Ambassador to the UN, Susan Rice, in her appearances on several television talk shows on Sunday, September 16, 2012. The contents of the talking points and Rice's comments in her public appearances generated significant controversy, including in Congress. As discussed in more detail below, the SSCI devoted considerable staff time and held three closed briefings for Members to address the Benghazi talking points issue.

The final, unclassified version of the CIA talking points, as provided to HPSCI on September 15, 2012, read as follows:

—The currently available information suggests that the demonstrations in Benghazi were spontaneously inspired by the protests at the US Embassy in Cairo and evolved into a direct assault against the US diplomatic post in Benghazi and subsequently its annex. There are indications that extremists participated in the violent demonstrations.

—This assessment may change as additional information is collected and analyzed as currently available information continues to be evaluated.

—The investigation is ongoing and the US Government is working with Libyan authorities to bring to justice those responsible for the deaths of US citizens.

---

[136] ABC News, "White House Benghazi Emails," accessed December 3, 2013, http://abcnews.go.com/images/Politics/white-house-benghazi-emails.pdf

SSCI Actions to Review the Talking Points

The SSCI conducted two closed, on-the-record sessions and one unrecorded session regarding the Benghazi talking points with the General Counsel of the ODNI, Robert Litt. Two similar on-the-record sessions occurred on January 3, 2013, the first with Litt and Chairman Feinstein and the second with Litt and Vice Chairman Chambliss, due to scheduling conflicts. Limited IC and SSCI staff were present at each session, but the transcript was made available to all SSCI members and staff. During the January 3 sessions, Litt went through the evolution of what he said were eleven different drafts of the talking points, starting on September 14 through the final version on September 15, 2012. He provided a summary document he created showing the changes made to each draft, without email time stamps and sender/recipient information because the Administration, claiming privilege, would not provide the Committee the opportunity to look at the actual emails. Members were not allowed to keep that handout, but staff were allowed to take notes.

A third Members-only session with Litt, which was not recorded, took place on February 26, 2013. During that session, Litt shared with Members copies of nearly 100 pages of emails associated with the interagency coordination process that took place in drafting the talking points. (Redacted versions of these emails were then made public by the Administration on May 15, 2013.) Litt also shared details about which individuals or agencies made changes to the points, when those changes occurred, and the nature of the changes. Members had to return the copies of the emails to Litt at the end of the briefing. Staff access to this briefing was strictly limited to both the Majority and Minority Staff Directors plus one additional staffer per side.

Members also asked questions about the talking points in open and closed hearings of the SSCI on multiple occasions, and staff submitted several formal questions for the record and informal inquiries to the IC about the issue. In some cases, the testimony of senior IC officials about the talking points was poorly informed or confusing, creating further uncertainty among Members and staff. Chairman Feinstein and Vice Chairman Chambliss also wrote to the DNI on two occasions—December 4, 2012, and January 30, 2013—specifically requesting full documentation on the changes made to the talking points.

This Committee faced significant resistance from the Administration in getting access to the emails and documentation that Mr. Litt ultimately provided on February 26, 2013, and that were then made public—in redacted form—on May 15, 2013. This resistance was apparently based, in part, on Executive branch concerns related to executive privilege and the deliberative process which appeared to evaporate when the emails were made public. However, it also served to exacerbate the controversy surrounding the talking points, prolonged media and public speculation, and raised questions of trust of the IC as Members attempted to extract information. This matter could have been mitigated much sooner if the Executive branch had promptly provided the email documentation that was ultimately given to SSCI on February 26th and made public on May 15th.

Analysis of the Talking Points

Below is the timeline of the twelve changes to the CIA talking points, as assembled from the 100 pages of emails made public by the Administration on May 15, 2013.[137] The timeline is in 12-point font to facilitate comparison to the publicly available summary document about the creation of the CIA talking points, which was created by Robert Litt.[138]

1) Fri., Sept. 14th 2012, 11:15 a.m.—written by Director, CIA Office of Terrorism Analysis

- We believe based on currently available information that the attacks in Benghazi were spontaneously inspired by the protests at the US Embassy in Cairo and evolved into a direct assault against the US Consulate and subsequently its annex.
- The crowd almost certainly was a mix of individuals from across many sectors of Libyan society. That being said, we do know that Islamic extremists with ties to al-Qa'ida participated in the attack.
- Initial press reporting linked the attack to Ansar al-Sharia. The group has since released a statement that the [sic] its leadership did not order the attacks, but did not deny that some of its members were involved. Ansar al-Sharia's facebook page aims to spread *sharia* in Libya and emphasizes the need for jihad to counter what it views as false interpretations of Islam, according to an open source study.

---

[137] Emails on CIA Talking Points, accessed December 5, 2013, http://abcnews.go.com/images/Politics/white-house-benghazi-emails.pdf
[138] ABC News, "CIA Benghazi Talking Points Timeline," accessed December 5, 2013, http://abcnews.go.com/images/Politics/Benghazi%20Talking%20Points%20Timeline.pdf

- The wide availability of weapons and experienced fighters in Libya almost certainly contributed to the lethality of the attacks.
- Since April, there have been at least five other attacks against foreign interests in Benghazi by unidentified assailants, including the June attack against the British Ambassador's convoy. We cannot rule out that individuals had previously surveilled the US facilities, also contributing to the efficacy of the attacks.
- We are working with Libyan authorities and intelligence partners in an effort to help bring to justice those responsible for the deaths of US citizens.

2) 12:23 p.m.—addition made by CIA's Office of General Counsel

- We believe based on currently available information that the attacks in Benghazi were spontaneously inspired by the protests at the US Embassy in Cairo and evolved into a direct assault against the US Consulate and subsequently its annex. This assessment may change as additional information is collected and analyzed and currently available information continues to be evaluated.
- The crowd almost certainly was a mix of individuals from across many sectors of Libyan society. That being said, we do know that Islamic extremists with ties to al-Qa'ida participated in the attack.
- Initial press reporting linked the attack to Ansar al-Sharia. The group has since released a statement that the [sic] its leadership did not order the attacks, but did not deny that some of its members were involved. Ansar al-Sharia's facebook page aims to spread *sharia* in Libya and emphasizes the need for jihad to counter what it views as false interpretations of Islam, according to an open source study.
- The wide availability of weapons and experienced fighters in Libya almost certainly contributed to the lethality of the attacks.
- Since April, there have been at least five other attacks against foreign interests in Benghazi by unidentified assailants, including the June attack of the British Ambassador's convoy. We cannot rule out that individuals had previously surveilled the US facilities, also contributing to the efficacy of the attacks.
- We are working with Libyan authorities and intelligence partners in an effort to help bring to justice those responsible for the deaths of US citizens.

3) 4:42 p.m.—edits made by CIA's (1) Office of Public Affairs & (2) Congressional Affairs

- The ~~We believe based on~~ currently available information suggests that the demonstrations ~~attacks~~ in Benghazi were spontaneously inspired by the protests at the US Embassy in Cairo and evolved into a direct assault against the US Consulate and subsequently its annex. This assessment may change as additional information is collected and analyzed and currently available information continues to be evaluated. On 10 September we warned of social media reports calling for a demonstration in front of the Embassy and that jihadists were threatening to break into the Embassy.

- The crowd almost certainly was a mix of individuals from across many sectors of Libyan society. The investigation is on-going as to who is responsible. That being said, we do know that Islamic extremists ~~with ties to al-Qa'ida~~ participated in the ~~attack~~ violent demonstrations.
- Initial press reporting linked the attack to Ansar al-Sharia. The group has since released a statement that ~~the~~ its leadership did not order the attacks, but did not deny that some of its members were involved. Ansar al-Sharia's Facebook page aims to spread sharia in Libya and emphasizes the need for jihad to counter what it views as false interpretations of Islam, according to an open source study.
- The wide availability of weapons and experienced fighters in Libya almost certainly contributed to the lethality of the attacks.
- The Agency has produced numerous pieces on the threat of extremists linked to al-Qaeda in Benghazi and eastern Libya. These noted that, since April, there have been at least five other attacks against foreign interests in Benghazi by unidentified assailants, including the June attack against the British Ambassador's convoy. We cannot rule out that individuals had previously surveilled the US facilities, also contributing to the efficacy of the attacks.
- The US Government is ~~We are~~ working with Libyan authorities and intelligence partners in an effort to help bring to justice those responsible for the deaths of US citizens.

4) 5:09 p.m.—edits made by CIA Deputy Director Mike Morell before being sent outside CIA for first time

- The currently available information suggests that the demonstrations in Benghazi were spontaneously inspired by the protests at the US Embassy in Cairo and evolved into a direct assault against the US Consulate and subsequently its annex. This assessment may change as additional information is collected and analyzed and currently available information continues to be evaluated. On 10 September we warned of social media reports calling for a demonstration in front of the Embassy and that jihadists were threatening to break into the Embassy.
- The crowd almost certainly was a mix of individuals from across many sectors of Libyan society. The investigation is on-going as to who is responsible for the violence. That being said, we do know that Islamic extremists participated in the violent demonstrations.
- Initial press reporting linked the attack to Ansar al-Sharia. The group has since released a statement that its leadership did not order the attacks, but did not deny that some of its members were involved. Ansar al-Sharia's Facebook page aims to spread sharia in Libya

and emphasizes the need for jihad to counter what it views as false interpretations of Islam, according to an open source study.

- The wide availability of weapons and experienced fighters in Libya almost certainly contributed to the lethality of the attacks.
- The Agency has produced numerous pieces on the threat of extremists linked to al-Qaeda in Benghazi and eastern Libya. These noted that, since April, there have been at least five other attacks against foreign interests in Benghazi by unidentified assailants, including the June attack against the British Ambassador's convoy. We cannot rule out that individuals had previously surveilled the US facilities, also contributing to the efficacy of the attacks.
- The US Government is working with Libyan authorities and intelligence partners in an effort to help bring to justice those responsible for the deaths of US citizens.

5) 6:21 p.m.—edit made by Tommy Vietor, Spokesman for the National Security Staff

- The currently available information suggests that the demonstrations in Benghazi were spontaneously inspired by the protests at the US Embassy in Cairo and evolved into a direct assault against the US Consulate and subsequently its annex. This assessment may change as additional information is collected and analyzed and currently available information continues to be evaluated. On 10 September we warned of social media reports calling for a demonstration in front of Embassy Cairo and that jihadists were threatening to break into the Embassy.
- The crowd almost certainly was a mix of individuals from across many sectors of Libyan society. The investigation is on-going as to who is responsible for the violence. That being said, we do know that Islamic extremists participated in the violent demonstrations.
- Initial press reporting linked the attack to Ansar al-Sharia. The group has since released a statement that its leadership did not order the attacks, but did not deny that some of its members were involved. Ansar al-Sharia's Facebook page aims to spread sharia in Libya and emphasizes the need for jihad to counter what it views as false interpretations of Islam, according to an open source study.
- The wide availability of weapons and experienced fighters in Libya almost certainly contributed to the lethality of the attacks.
- The Agency has produced numerous pieces on the threat of extremists linked to al-Qaeda in Benghazi and eastern Libya. These noted that, since April, there have been at least five other attacks against foreign interests in Benghazi by unidentified assailants, including the June attack against the British Ambassador's convoy. We cannot rule out that individuals had previously surveilled the US facilities, also contributing to the efficacy of the attacks.

- The US Government is working with Libyan authorities and intelligence partners in an effort to help bring to justice those responsible for the deaths of US citizens.

6) 6:41 p.m.—edits made by Shawn Turner, ODNI Spokesman

- The currently available information suggests that the demonstrations in Benghazi were spontaneously inspired by the protests at the US Embassy in Cairo and evolved into a direct assault against the US Consulate and subsequently its annex. This assessment may change as additional information is collected and analyzed and currently available information continues to be evaluated. On 10 September we notified Embassy Cairo ~~warned~~ of social media reports calling for a demonstration and encouraging ~~in front of the Embassy Cairo and that~~ jihadists ~~were threatening~~ to break into the Embassy.
- The crowd almost certainly was a mix of individuals from across many sectors of Libyan society. The investigation is on-going as to who is responsible for the violence. That being said, we do know that Islamic extremists participated in the violent demonstrations.
- Initial press reporting linked the attack to Ansar al-Sharia. The group has since released a statement that its leadership did not order the attacks, but did not deny that some of its members were involved. Ansar al-Sharia's Facebook page aims to spread sharia in Libya and emphasizes the need for jihad to counter what it views as false interpretations of Islam, according to an open source study.
- The wide availability of weapons and experienced fighters in Libya almost certainly contributed to the lethality of the attacks.
- The Agency has produced numerous pieces on the threat of extremists linked to al-Qaeda in Benghazi and eastern Libya. These noted that, since April, there have been at least five other attacks against foreign interests in Benghazi by unidentified assailants, including the June attack against the British Ambassador's convoy. We cannot rule out that individuals had previously surveilled the US facilities, also contributing to the efficacy of the attacks.
- The US Government is working with Libyan authorities and intelligence partners in an effort to help bring to justice those responsible for the deaths of US citizens.

7) 6:52 p.m.—edits made by Tommy Vietor on behalf of Assistant to the President for Homeland Security and Counterterrorism, John Brennan

- The currently available information suggests that the demonstrations in Benghazi were spontaneously inspired by the protests at the US Embassy in Cairo and evolved into a direct assault against the US Consulate and subsequently its annex. This assessment may change as additional information is collected and analyzed and currently available information continues to be evaluated. On 10 September we notified Embassy Cairo of social media reports calling for a demonstration and encouraging jihadists to break into the Embassy.

- ~~The crowd almost certainly was a mix of individuals from across many sectors of Libyan society.~~ The investigation is on-going as to who is responsible for the violence, although the crowd almost certainly was a mix of individuals. ~~That being said,~~ We do know that Islamic extremists participated in the violent demonstrations.
- Initial press reporting linked the attack to Ansar al-Sharia. The group has since released a statement that its leadership did not order the attacks, but did not deny that some of its members were involved. Ansar al-Sharia's Facebook page aims to spread sharia in Libya and emphasizes the need for jihad to counter what it views as false interpretations of Islam, according to an open source study.
- The wide availability of weapons and experienced fighters in Libya almost certainly contributed to the lethality of the attacks.
- The Agency has produced numerous pieces on the threat of extremists linked to al-Qaeda in Benghazi and eastern Libya. These noted that, since April, there have been at least five other attacks against foreign interests in Benghazi by unidentified assailants, including the June attack against the British Ambassador's convoy. We cannot rule out that individuals had previously surveilled the US facilities, also contributing to the efficacy of the attacks.
- The US Government is working with Libyan authorities and intelligence partners in an effort to help bring to justice those responsible for the deaths of US citizens.

8) 8:58 p.m.—first two edits suggested by FBI, all made by CIA's Office of Public Affairs

- The currently available information suggests that the demonstrations in Benghazi were spontaneously inspired by the protests at the US Embassy in Cairo and evolved into a direct assault against the US Consulate and subsequently its annex. This assessment may change as additional information is collected and analyzed and currently available information continues to be evaluated. On 10 September the Agency ~~we~~ notified Embassy Cairo of social media reports calling for a demonstration and encouraging jihadists to break into the Embassy.
- The investigation is on-going as to who is responsible for the violence, although the crowd almost certainly was a mix of individuals. That being said, there are indications ~~we do know~~ that Islamic extremists participated in the violent demonstrations.
- ~~Initial press presorting linked the attack to Ansar al-Sharia. The group has since released a statement that its leadership did not order the attacks, but did not deny that some of its members were involved. Ansar al-Sharia's Facebook page aims to spread sharia in Libya and emphasizes the need for jihad to counter what it views as false interpretations of Islam, according to an open source study.~~

- The wide availability of weapons and experienced fighters in Libya almost certainly contributed to the lethality of the attacks.
- The Agency has produced numerous pieces on the threat of extremists linked to al-Qaeda in Benghazi and eastern Libya. ~~These noted that,~~ Since April, there have been at least five other attacks against foreign interests in Benghazi by unidentified assailants, including the June attack against the British Ambassador's convoy. We cannot rule out that individuals had previously surveilled the US facilities, also contributing to the efficacy of the attacks.
- The US Government is working with Libyan authorities and intelligence partners in an effort to help bring to justice those responsible for the deaths of US citizens.

9) Saturday, Sept. 15th 9:45 a.m.—edits made by CIA Deputy Director Mike Morell

- The currently available information suggests that the demonstrations in Benghazi were spontaneously inspired by the protests at the US Embassy in Cairo and evolved into a direct assault against the US Consulate and subsequently its annex.
- This assessment may change as additional information is collected and analyzed and currently available information continues to be evaluated. ~~On 10 September the Agency notified Embassy Cairo of social media reports calling for a demonstration and encouraging jihadists to break into the Embassy.~~
- The investigation is on-going, and ~~as to who is responsible for the violence, although the crowd almost certainly was a mix of individuals. That being said, there are indications that Islamic extremists participated in the violent demonstrations.~~
- ~~The wide availability of weapons and experienced fighters in Libya almost certainly contribute to the lethality of the attacks.~~
- ~~The Agency has produced numerous pieces on the threat of extremists linked to al-Qaeda in Benghazi and eastern Libya. Since April, there have been at least five other attacks against foreign interests in Benghazi by unidentified assailants, including the June attack against the British Ambassador's convoy. We cannot rule out that individuals had previously surveilled the US facilities, also contributing to the efficacy of the attacks.~~ the US Government is working with Libyan authorities ~~and intelligence partners in an effort~~ to ~~help~~ bring to justice those responsible for the deaths of US citizens.

10) 11:08 a.m.—edits made by CIA Deputy Director Mike Morell

- The currently available information suggests that the demonstrations in Benghazi were spontaneously inspired by the protests at the US Embassy in Cairo and evolved into a direct assault against the US Consulate and subsequently its annex. There are indications that extremists participated in the violent demonstrations.

- This assessment may change as additional information is collected and analyzed and as currently available information continues to be evaluated.
- The investigation is on-going, and the US Government is working with Libyan authorities to bring to justice those responsible for the deaths US citizens.

11) 11:25 a.m.—edits made by Deputy National Security Adviser Ben Rhodes

- The currently available information suggests that the demonstrations in Benghazi were spontaneously inspired by the protests at the US Embassy in Cairo and evolved into a direct assault against the US diplomatic post in Benghazi ~~Consulate~~ and subsequently its annex. There are indications that extremists participated in the violent demonstrations.
- This assessment may change as additional information is collected and analyzed and as currently available information continues to be evaluated.
- The investigation is on-going, and the US Government is working with Libyan authorities to bring to justice those responsible for the deaths US citizens.

12) 11:26 a.m.—edits made by State Department official Jake Sullivan

- The currently available information suggests that the demonstrations in Benghazi were spontaneously inspired by the protests at the US Embassy in Cairo and evolved into a direct assault against the US diplomatic post in Benghazi and subsequently its annex. There are indications that extremists participated in the violent demonstrations.
- This assessment may change as additional information is collected and analyzed and as currently available information continues to be evaluated.
- The investigation is on-going, and the US Government is working with Libyan authorities to bring to justice those responsible for the deaths of US citizens.

APPENDIX II: Unclassified Timeline of the Benghazi Attacks

There were effectively three different phases/attacks against the U.S. Temporary Mission Facility and the CIA Annex in Benghazi on September 11-12, 2012, as described below.[139]

1. Attack on the U.S. Temporary Mission Facility at Approximately 9:40 p.m.

9:42 p.m.   Video footage shows—and the Accountability Review Board also found—that, at 9:42 p.m., a local police vehicle stationed outside the Temporary Mission Facility withdrew as soon as armed attackers advanced toward the U.S. compound.

Dozens of attackers easily gained access to the TMF by scaling and then opening the front vehicle gate.

(Over the course of the entire attack on the Mission facility, at least 60 different attackers entered the U.S. compound.)

Ambassador Chris Stevens was in the residence of the Main Building ("Building C"), along with a Diplomatic Security agent, and Information Management Officer Sean Smith. The three of them proceeded to the "safe area" in the building.

DS personnel contacted CIA personnel at the Annex to ask for assistance.

9:45 p.m.   After entering the Mission facility, the attackers used diesel fuel to set fire to the barracks/guard house of the Libyan 17th February Brigade militia, which served as a security force provided by the host nation for the Mission compound, and then proceeded towards the main buildings of the compound.

The attackers then used diesel fuel to set the Main Building ablaze where Ambassador Stevens was secured in the "safe area." Thick smoke rapidly filled the entire structure. The attackers moved unimpeded throughout the compound, entering and exiting buildings at will.

---

[139] Times are approximate and local to Libya.

10:00 p.m.   A DS agent began leading the Ambassador and Sean Smith toward the emergency escape window to escape the smoke. Nearing unconsciousness himself, the agent opened the emergency escape window and crawled out. He then realized he had become separated from the Ambassador and Sean Smith in the smoke, so he reentered and searched the building multiple times.

The DS agent, suffering from severe smoke inhalation, climbed a ladder to the roof where he radioed the other DS agents for assistance.

10:03 p.m.   The CIA security team left the Annex for the Mission compound after team members secured heavy weapons.

10:10 p.m.   Security team members started arriving at the Mission facility and made their way onto the compound in the face of enemy fire.

10:30 p.m.   In their armored vehicle, other DS agents drove from Building B to assist the agent on the roof of Building C who had searched for the Ambassador and Mr. Smith. After numerous attempts, they found Mr. Smith, who was deceased.

The CIA security team from the Annex and some 17th February Brigade members pushed back the attackers and secured a perimeter around the Main Building, and the security team joined in the search for the Ambassador.

11:10 p.m.   An unarmed, unmanned DoD surveillance aircraft arrived over the Mission compound and soon after detected a roadblock several blocks east of the Mission facility. During this time, State and CIA personnel re-entered the burning compound numerous times in an attempt to locate Ambassador Stevens, but to no avail.

11:15 p.m.   The combined CIA and DS security team made a final search for the Ambassador before leaving for the Annex in two separate armored vehicles. One vehicle encountered heavy fire as it ran a roadblock several blocks east of the Mission compound.

11:30 p.m. All U.S. personnel, except for the missing U.S. Ambassador, arrived at the CIA Annex, which was approximately two kilometers away. Sean Smith's body was also taken to the Annex.

2. Attack on the CIA Annex from Approximately 11:56 p.m. until 1:00 a.m.

11:56 p.m. Sporadic arms fire and rocket-propelled grenades (RPGs) were fired at the Annex. Over the next hour, the Annex took sporadic small arms fire and RPG rounds, the security team returned fire, and the attackers dispersed.

1:00 a.m. Local Libyans found the Ambassador at the Mission Facility and brought him to a local hospital. Despite attempts to revive him, Ambassador Stevens had no heartbeat and had perished from smoke inhalation.

1:15 a.m. A seven-man reinforcement team of additional U.S. security personnel from Tripoli landed at the Benghazi airport and began to negotiate with the local Libyan militias for transportation and a security convoy to the Annex.

4:30 a.m. The security team from Tripoli departed the airport for the Annex after more than three hours of negotiations and communications with Libyan officials.

3. Final Attack on the CIA Annex at Approximately 5:15 a.m.

5:04 a.m. The security team from Tripoli arrived at the Annex.

5:15 a.m. Mortar rounds, small-arms fire, and RPGs began to hit the Annex. Tyrone Woods and Glen Doherty were killed when they took direct mortar fire as they engaged the enemy from the roof of the Annex. The mortar fire also seriously injured one other security officer and one DS special agent, necessitating the evacuation of the Annex. That attack lasted only 11 minutes, then dissipated.

6:00 a.m.   A heavily-armed Libyan militia unit arrived to help evacuate the Annex of all U.S. personnel to the airport.

6:33 a.m.   U.S. personnel left the Annex for the airport.

7:30 a.m.   The first plane of U.S. personnel evacuated from Benghazi to Tripoli.

10:00 a.m.   The second plane of U.S. personnel evacuated from Benghazi to Tripoli. This flight included the bodies of the four dead Americans.

APPENDIX III: Locations of Temporary Mission Facility & Annex

Source: NGA, November, 2012

APPENDIX IV: Map from September 5, 2012, AFRICOM Report

(U) Report Title: *"Libya: Extremism in Libya Past, Present, and Future."*

This page intentionally left blank.

ADDITIONAL MAJORITY VIEWS

Overview

The Majority[140] believes that the terrorist attacks against U.S. personnel at the Temporary Mission Facility and the Annex in Benghazi, Libya, on September 11 and 12, 2012, were likely preventable based on the known security shortfalls at the U.S. Mission and the significant strategic (although not tactical) warnings from the Intelligence Community (IC) about the deteriorating security situation in Libya. The Majority also believes, however, that the Benghazi attacks have been the subject of misinformed speculation and accusations long after the basic facts of the attacks have been determined, thereby distracting attention from more important concerns: the tragic deaths of four brave Americans, the hunt for their attackers, efforts by the U.S. Government to avoid future attacks, and the future of the U.S.-Libya relationship.

The Majority would like to commend our Republican colleagues on the Committee who supported this report for their earnest and thorough efforts with us to find out what really happened in Benghazi before, during, and after the attacks, despite the swirling controversy and pressures. To produce this report, we worked together on a bipartisan basis to dispel the many factual inaccuracies and conspiracy theories related to the Benghazi attacks so that the public would have a fair and accurate accounting of the events.

We would also like to express our appreciation for the dedication and professionalism of the workforce of the IC which, as noted in a key finding in this report, provided strategic warning about the deteriorating security situation in Libya and the threat to U.S. interests there in the months prior to the attacks in Benghazi.

The Talking Points Controversy

Perhaps no issue related to Benghazi has been as mischaracterized as the unclassified talking points prepared by the Central Intelligence Agency (CIA) at the request of the House Permanent Select Committee on Intelligence (HPSCI) and provided to HPSCI, this Committee, and Administration officials on September 15,

---

[140] For the purposes of this report, and this Committee, the Majority includes Independent Senator Angus King.

2012. The Majority notes that the controversy over the CIA talking points consumed a regrettable and disproportionate amount of time and energy during the Committee's substantive review of the Benghazi attacks.

1. *The Talking Points Were Flawed But Mostly Accurate*

The Majority believes that the CIA talking points were flawed but—as discussed in the report—painted a mostly accurate picture of the IC's analysis of the Benghazi attacks **at that time, in an unclassified form and without compromising the nascent investigation of the attacks** by the Federal Bureau of Investigation (FBI). In retrospect, the talking points could have and should have been clearer. As discussed below, omissions and wording choices contributed to significant controversy and confusion, as did an erroneous reference to "demonstrations." In addition, the Administration was slow to provide details explaining the drafting and editing process that produced the talking points. Speculation and conspiracy theories about the details could have been mitigated if the factual record of how the talking points were produced was provided sooner to this Committee and to the public.

Officials in the Executive Branch and Members of Congress also added to the confusion in the days after September 11, 2012, by inconsistently characterizing the events in Benghazi, even though the President referred to them as "attacks" and "acts of terror" on September 12, 2012.[141] Administration officials provided vague and sometimes conflicting characterizations of the events in some instances. Members of Congress also lent support to the narrative of a protest gone awry for days following the attack. For example, in a September 22, 2012, resolution honoring the four Americans who died, the Senate unanimously adopted the narrative that the violence in Benghazi "coincided with an attack on the United States Embassy in Cairo, Egypt, which was **also** swarmed by an angry mob of protesters on September 11, 2012."[142]

2. *Confusion from Use of the Term "Terrorists" vs. "Extremists"*

A key point of contention was that the final talking points referred to "extremists" rather than "terrorists." IC analysts and senior leaders such as former

---

[141] "Remarks by the President on the Deaths of U.S. Embassy Staff in Libya," The Rose Garden, September 12, 2012.
[142] S. Res. 588 (2012). Emphasis added.

CIA Director David Petraeus testified to the Committee that when describing attackers, the word "extremist" was meant to imply that terrorist groups were involved – and, in fact, elements of the IC routinely use the term "Islamist extremists" when referring to al-Qaida and similar groups.[143] However, the assumption that these two terms would be seen by the public as interchangeable proved to be incorrect. "Extremists" and "terrorists" are not interchangeable terms. Some in the public, Congress, and the press interpreted the use of the word "extremist" as an attempt to downplay the role of terrorists in the Benghazi attacks. Through the course of our review, however, we found no evidence of any effort to downplay the role of terrorists in the Benghazi attacks.

3. The CIA Dropped the Term "Al-Qa'ida"

It is important to reiterate that the reference to "al-Qa'ida" included in early drafts of the talking points was removed by CIA staff, **not** by the White House or the FBI, as was incorrectly alleged by some members of Congress and the press. The reference was removed in an internal CIA draft **prior** to dissemination to the interagency process and prior to senior CIA leadership viewing the draft. These facts are corroborated by emails provided to the Committee on a "read and return" basis on February 26, 2013, and made public on May 15, 2013.

According to testimony before the Committee by General Counsel for the Director of National Intelligence (DNI) Robert Litt on February 26, 2013, the reference to "al-Qa'ida" was removed to protect intelligence sources and methods. This rationale was neither confirmed nor refuted in the emails provided. However, according to testimony by former CIA Director David Petraeus, when the talking points were drafted, classified sources and methods did exist that linked a specific terrorist group to the attack, but the IC did not yet have an unclassified factual basis for connecting the attacks to any group formally affiliated with or self-affiliated with al-Qa'ida.[144] In addition, the CIA staff who edited the points made changes eliminating "al-Qa'ida" and "Ansar al-Sharia" to ensure that the points contained no information that could either: (1) reveal intelligence sources and methods or (2) compromise the FBI investigation by prematurely attributing responsibility for the attacks to any one person or group, thereby pre-judging a

---

[143] Statement by David Petraeus, Former CIA Director, *Hearing with General David Petraeus Re: His Knowledge of the Attacks on U.S. Facilities in Benghazi, Libya*, November 16, 2012, p. 17, SSCI Document Tracking System.
[144] Ibid, p. 16-17.

potential prosecution and making it harder to charge other perpetrators in the future.[145]

4. *There Were No Protests in Benghazi*

We now know that the CIA's September 15, 2012, talking points were inaccurate in that they wrongly attributed the genesis of the Benghazi attacks to protests that became violent. However, as stated in the report, this characterization reflected the assessment by the IC of the information available at that time, which lacked sufficient intelligence and eyewitness statements to conclude that there were no protests. Further, it is important to remember that this early assessment was made in the context of approximately 40 protests around the globe against U.S. embassies and consulates in response to an inflammatory film. There were also other violent attacks against U.S. embassies and consulates in Egypt, Tunisia, Yemen and other cities around the world on or after September 11. According to CIA emails dated September 16, 2012, the then-Deputy Director of the CIA requested further information from CIA staff at Embassy Tripoli about whether there was countervailing evidence of protests that occurred prior to the attacks in Benghazi. It was not until September 24, 2012—eight days later—that the IC revised its assessment that there were no protests leading up to the attacks (*see* discussion in the main report under Finding #9 for bipartisan Committee views on the development of the intelligence picture after the attacks).

5. *The Talking Points Went Through the Normal Interagency Coordination Process*

The Majority concludes that the interagency coordination process on the talking points followed normal, but rushed coordination procedures and that there were no efforts by the White House or any other Executive Branch entities to

---

[145] According to the CIA, the talking points editors at the Agency were influenced by an email from an officer in the National Clandestine Service saying that the part of the original talking points stating that "we do know that Islamic extremists with ties to al-Qa'ida participated in the attack" implied complicity in the deaths of the Americans and therefore could compromise the FBI investigation. The CIA employee who drafted the first version of the points therefore agreed that because it was still unknown precisely who was responsible for the Benghazi attacks, the language of the third version of the talking points should be changed to say "we know that they [Islamic extremists] participated in the protests." Although the CIA personnel editing points did not make this change, "attack" in the second bullet was changed to "violent demonstrations," effectively accomplishing the same purpose. In addition, the word "attacks" in the first bullet of the talking points was changed to "demonstrations." The CIA staff editing the talking points also then deleted the mention in the second bullet of the extremists who participated having "ties to al-Qa'ida." *See* report from Michael J. Morell, "Lessons Learned from Formulation of Unclassified Talking Points re the Events in Benghazi, 11-12 September 2012," August 6, 2013, p. 4.

65

"cover-up" facts or make alterations for political purposes. Indeed, former CIA Director David Petraeus testified to the Committee on November 16, 2012, "They went through the normal process that talking points—unclassified public talking points—go through."[146] In fact, the purpose of the National Security Council (NSC) is to coordinate the many national security agencies of the government, especially when information about a terrorist attack is flowing in and being analyzed quickly—and the NSC used this role appropriately in the case of the talking points coordination. Furthermore, such coordination processes were also standardized, often at the urging of Congress, following the September 11, 2001, terrorist attacks with the explicit goal of reducing information "stovepipes" between and among agencies.

6. Conclusion

The Majority agrees that the process to create the talking points was not without problems, so we join our Republican colleagues in recommending—as we do in the report—that in responding to future requests for unclassified talking points from Congress, the IC should simply tell Congress which facts are unclassified and let Members of Congress provide additional context for the public. However, we sincerely hope that the public release of the emails on May 15, 2013, that describe the creation of the talking points, and the evidence presented in this report, will end the misinformed and unhelpful talking points controversy once and for all.

DIANNE FEINSTEIN
JOHN D. ROCKEFELLER IV
RON WYDEN
BARBARA A. MIKULSKI
MARK UDALL
MARK WARNER
MARTIN HEINRICH
ANGUS KING

---

[146] Statement by David Petraeus, Former CIA Director, *Hearing with General David Petraeus Re: His Knowledge of the Attacks on U.S. Facilities in Benghazi, Libya,* November 16, 2012, p. 24.

ADDITIONAL VIEWS OF VICE CHAIRMAN CHAMBLISS AND SENATORS BURR, RISCH, COATS, RUBIO, AND COBURN

Over a year has passed since the terrorist attacks on U.S. facilities in Benghazi, Libya, claimed the lives of four brave Americans—Glen Doherty, Sean Smith, Christopher Stevens, and Tyrone Woods. The Senate Select Committee on Intelligence endeavored to conduct a thorough and bipartisan review of the events and circumstances surrounding these attacks. The Committee's report, the *SSCI Review of Terrorist Attacks on U.S. Facilities in Benghazi, September 11-12, 2012,* offers findings and recommendations that we hope will improve intelligence collection and analysis, information sharing, and the physical security for Americans serving overseas in our diplomatic and intelligence facilities.

While the Committee has completed its report, important questions remain unanswered as a direct result of the Obama Administration's failure to provide the Committee with access to necessary documents and witnesses. We believe the Administration's lack of cooperation is directly contrary to its statutory obligation to keep the congressional intelligence committees fully and currently informed and has effectively obstructed the Committee's efforts to get to the ground truth with respect to these remaining questions. Too often, providing timely and complete information to Congress is viewed by the Administration as optional or an accommodation, rather than compliance with a statutory requirement. It is our view that the Committee should have held a vote to exercise its subpoena power to end this obstruction, once and for all, in the early stages of the review.

As we prepared these Additional Views, the Executive branch still has not provided all relevant documents to the Committee. Other documents have been provided to the Committee on a "read only" basis, meaning that the Committee was only permitted to view them for a limited period of time, while being supervised by the coordinating agency, and had to rely upon our notes when preparing the report. Significantly, key Executive branch witnesses who were directly involved in decisions that affected the ability of the United States to defend or respond to these attacks have declined our invitations to be interviewed by the Committee, even after being returned to full duty by the State Department. In other cases, the testimony provided to the Committee contradicted written documents we reviewed, or—as with some of the testimony by the Under Secretary of State for Management, Patrick Kennedy—was particularly specious.

We understand that mistakes can be made during the back-and-forth of oral testimony, but when that occurs, the Intelligence Community (IC) and the Executive branch have historically been quick to correct the record. Yet, we are still waiting for some of these troubling contradictions to be resolved. Further, in what is becoming an habitual refrain, the Administration has made repeated and spurious claims of the "executive" and "deliberative process" privileges, serving to deny information to the Committee that was otherwise relevant to our review. Similarly, information has been withheld from the Committee because of the "ongoing criminal investigation" into the attacks, in an apparent effort to shield certain government agencies from congressional oversight or potential embarrassment. We have also learned that the Federal Bureau of Investigation has developed significant information about the attacks and the suspected attackers that is not being shared with Congress, even where doing so would not in any way impact an ongoing investigation.

Complete Absence of Accountability

In the course of this review, we have come to the unavoidable conclusion that, for an event marked by significant failures, one of the biggest failures is the Administration's complete refusal or inability to attain accountability—from the attackers themselves and from those U.S. Government officials who made poor management decisions relating to the Benghazi facilities. This is not a charge we bring lightly, but it is one clearly substantiated by the facts. We recognize that sometimes circumstances are simply beyond our control, but the Benghazi attacks do not fall into this category of chance. Prior to the attacks, senior U.S. Government officials were aware of the deteriorating security situation and tenuous physical security of the Temporary Mission Facility in Benghazi, but did little, if anything, of consequence about it. The U.S. government personnel on the ground in Benghazi raised constant alarms in the months before September 2012. The combination of these alarms with the multitude of prior attacks in the Benghazi area should have spurred swift action by State Department officials in Washington. It did not. Many times, the lack of congressional funding is used by an Administration to downplay its own role or minimize responsibility; but in this case, this excuse simply cannot justify highly questionable management decisions. To date, in spite of legitimate questions about the actions of these senior officials raised by our own review, the reviews of other congressional committees, and the Accountability Review Board, not one person has faced disciplinary action of any consequence.

We believe the background of one senior State Department official made him uniquely situated to anticipate the potential for a terrorist attack on the Benghazi facilities. Prior to the 1998 East Africa Embassy bombings which killed 12 Americans, Under Secretary Kennedy was serving as the Assistant Secretary of State for Administration, and concurrently served as the Acting Assistant Secretary of State for Diplomatic Security. Coincidentally, some of the same failures identified by the report of the Accountability Review Board following the 1998 Embassy bombings were noted by the Benghazi Accountability Review Board. Mr. Kennedy later served in key positions in Iraq, in the immediate aftermath of the toppling of Saddam Hussein, and in the IC. The threat of terrorism, including against U.S. facilities, was not new to him, and given the security situation in Benghazi, the attacks could have been foreseen. Given the threat environment, Mr. Kennedy should have used better judgment and should be held accountable.

We are equally disturbed by the Administration's ongoing failure to secure justice and accountability for those responsible for these attacks. Despite the President's promise, not a single suspected attacker is in custody. Ahmed Abu Khattala, whom the press reports has been charged by the United States for his lead role in the attacks, continues to live freely in Libya while giving taunting interviews to major media outlets. Yet, inexplicably, U.S. diplomacy cannot seem to secure his capture so he can be detained and fully interrogated before any criminal proceedings are initiated. Other leading suspects, such as Faraj al-Chalabi and Ali Ani al-Harzi, also remain free, including after failed diplomatic efforts by the Secretary of State relating to al-Harzi's capture and interrogation. As we discuss later in these views, the President's failure to develop a clear, cogent detention and interrogation policy and his refusal to yield on sending new terrorists to Guantanamo Bay have had—and will continue to have—far-reaching consequences for our national security, as exemplified by the events relating to Benghazi. There simply is no justification, not even an ill-conceived campaign promise, for not doing more to capture and interrogate terrorists who caused the deaths of four Americans. The United States can and should do better. We have heard the excuse that these terrorists cannot be captured because Libya is a dangerous operating environment. Yet, the same Administration offering this excuse somehow managed to recently capture al-Qa'ida operative Abu Anas al-Libi in Tripoli, briefly interrogate him, and bring him to the United States for prosecution for his role in the 1998 Embassy bombings. We believe a similar result is possible here, but only if the U.S. Government more aggressively pursues justice for these attacks against our nation.

Manipulating the Facts

When American citizens are murdered in terrorist attacks against our nation, we believe the Executive branch has a particular obligation, beyond statutory requirements, to openly and fully cooperate with congressional efforts to investigate and understand these matters, no matter how potentially embarrassing or inconvenient. That certainly has not been the case here. From the beginning, the Administration's handling of the Benghazi attacks has been a source of confusion to Congress, the American people, other nations, and—most significantly—the families of those killed in Benghazi. From the refusal to clearly explain the decisions by, and interactions of, the President, the Secretary of Defense, and the Secretary of State on the night of the attacks to the talking points fiasco, the Administration's response has been notable for its deficiencies. Many of us were frustrated and astounded by the great pains the Administration took after the attacks to avoid the clear linkage of what happened in Benghazi to the threat of international terrorism. Contrary to the long-standing commitment of the Office of the Director of National Intelligence (ODNI) and the Central Intelligence Agency (CIA) to provide timely information to the Committee following any terrorist attack or attempted attack, we were given neither prompt nor adequate information about the Benghazi attacks. Instead, we were subjected to Sunday news programs, carefully crafted speeches, and delayed briefings—all designed to label the terrorist attacks as violent demonstrations spontaneously inspired by an obscure anti-Muslim film that has long since been forgotten.

Maybe we would be less skeptical if there were not so many examples of this Administration downplaying the very real threat of international terrorism. The Fort Hood terrorist attack by Nidal Hasan was labeled "workplace violence," despite Hasan's email communications with al-Qa'ida in the Arabian Peninsula cleric, Anwar al-Aulaqi, in the months before he opened fire, killing 13 and wounding 32 military and civilian personnel in 2009. Another Aulaqi protégé, Umar Farouk Abdulmutallab, was treated as an ordinary criminal and given *Miranda* warnings, despite being captured after failing to detonate plastic explosives on a Northwest Airlines flight over Detroit on December 25, 2009. Then there was Faisal Shahzad, the incompetent Times Square bomber, whose car bomb failed to detonate in May 2010. The Administration tried to spin Shahzad as a one-off lone wolf until the media discovered he had traveled to Pakistan for five months and trained with the Pakistani Taliban. As with Benghazi, the Administration's obligation to provide information to Congress about those cases seemed to be superseded by a desire to script the message that al-Qa'ida had been decimated or to protect a criminal investigation in spite of equally vital intelligence prerogatives.

The Talking Points

The obstruction faced by the Committee during its review is epitomized by the months-long saga involving the CIA's Benghazi talking points. In the immediate aftermath of September 11th, the Committee began asking the IC who was likely responsible for the attacks and what the intelligence was indicating. At the same time, the House Permanent Select Committee on Intelligence requested unclassified talking points from the CIA that could be used by Members in responding to press inquiries. Rather than simply provide Congress with the best intelligence and on-the-ground assessments, the Administration chose to try to frame the story in a way that minimized any connection to terrorism. Before the Benghazi attacks—in the lead-up to the 2012 presidential election, the Administration had continued to script the narrative that al-Qa'ida had been decimated and was on the run. The Benghazi terrorist attacks inconveniently, and overwhelmingly, interfered with this fictitious and politically-motivated storyline. Thus, the story as told through the talking points and repeated on the Sunday talk shows became one of a protest or demonstration gone awry, rather than an act of terrorism against the United States by individuals with ties to al-Qa'ida. Until the forthright testimony of the Director of the National Counterterrorism Center (NCTC) on September 19, 2012,[147] no one in the Administration—from the President[148] on down—had publicly called Benghazi the terrorist attack it clearly was. Yet, when the Administration was questioned after the NCTC Director's

---

[147] Matthew G. Olsen, Director of NCTC, *Testimony before the Senate Homeland Security and Governmental Affairs Committee during Hearing on Homeland Threats and Agency Responses,* September 19, 2012.
[148] In his Rose Garden speech the day after the Benghazi attacks, the President passed up at least ten opportunities to clearly identify the Benghazi attacks as terrorist attacks. Instead, he chose to use the following: "killed in an attack," "outrageous and shocking attack," "killers who attacked," "this type of senseless violence," "these brutal acts," "this attack," "fought back against the attackers," "this attack in Benghazi," "this terrible act," and "those of their attackers." His statement—"No acts of terror will ever shake the resolve of this great nation"—does nothing to resolve this shortcoming, as its placement in this speech simply creates ambiguity in whether it refers to the previously cited terrorist attacks on September 11, 2001, or is meant to include the Benghazi terrorist attacks as well.

testimony, IC officials, including the Director and Deputy Director of the CIA, said they knew instantly during the attacks that it was terrorism.[149]

As the Committee began to receive intelligence relating to the attacks, it became clear that the narrative conveyed through the talking points and during the Sunday talk shows did not stand up to scrutiny. We now know that the talking points, as originally drafted by the CIA, included the words "al-Qa'ida," "Ansar al-Sharia," and "attacks," and spoke of other attacks against foreign interests in Benghazi. There was no mention of a protest gone awry outside the Temporary Mission Facility. Yet, through an "interagency process" that specifically included coordination with and by the White House, the message was recast to downplay or eliminate these references and minimize any potential embarrassment to the State Department for its failure to heed earlier security warnings.

Rather than openly engage with the Committee on how the talking points were drafted, the Administration resisted repeated Committee efforts to learn who was involved and what changes were made, including by imposing unreasonable restrictions on Member and staff access to the same information about the talking points that would eventually be released to the public. Not until the nomination of John Brennan to be the next Director of the CIA was pending before the Committee, did the Administration even consider addressing the Committee's requests, albeit still with resistance. In response to specific requests by the Committee for the full paper trail, the emails documenting the changes in the talking points drafts, they chose to provide a re-creation of the drafts by the ODNI and simply on a "read only" basis. These conditions meant there was no opportunity for in-depth, ongoing exploration by Members or staff of the paper trail. As the Administration well knows, the "read only" practice is often used to "check the box" on providing information to Congress, but to do so in a way that is simply not helpful to congressional oversight as it denies ready and complete access to documents. It took seven months before these emails were finally disclosed in full to Congress, and to the public in redacted form.

Compounding this resistance, no effort was made to correct the record when, during testimony before the Committee in late 2012, the Acting Director of the CIA emphatically stated that the talking points were sent to the White House "for

---

[149] *See, e.g.,* SSCI Transcript, *Hearing on the Attacks in Benghazi,* November 15, 2012, pp. 55, 62, 65, and 116-118; and SSCI Transcript, *Hearing with General David Petraeus Re: His Knowledge of the Attacks on U.S. Facilities in Benghazi, Libya,* November 16, 2012, pp. 17 and 83-84.

their awareness, not for their coordination."[150] The emails, which the Committee received later, clearly show that the White House was, from the earliest moments, asked to "coordinate" on the talking points.[151] This may seem, to some, like a distinction without a difference, but in the world of Federal government interactions, "coordination" carries with it a level of involvement and responsibility to overrule or influence that is not present when information is conveyed simply "for awareness." The measure of White House influence can be seen in a September 15, 2012, email[152] from then-CIA Director David Petraeus acknowledging that, in spite of his own misgivings, the final content of the talking points was the "[National Security Staff's] call, to be sure." In contrast, the Acting Director's testimony perpetuated the myth that the White House played no part in the drafting or editing of the talking points. Today, it remains unclear exactly what was discussed during the Deputies Committee meeting that resulted in the final version of the talking points—or even who was present besides the Acting Director of the CIA, who actually made the edits. These are basic questions that should have been readily answered in the interests of transparency and accountability.

Disturbing Lack of Cooperation by the State Department

As the Committee attempted to piece together key events before, during, and after the attacks, we faced the most significant and sustained resistance from the State Department in obtaining documents, access to witnesses, and responses to questions. The Committee does, on occasion, deal with "jurisdictional" obstacles that bureaucratically arise when we seek information relevant to an intelligence matter, simply because the holder of the information is not an element of the IC. Our review of the Benghazi attacks was no different. Even though the attacks involved IC employees and the CIA Annex and it was CIA personnel who came to the aid of the personnel at the Temporary Mission Facility, the State Department swiftly asserted questionable jurisdictional objections and resisted full cooperation with our review. We surmise that this lack of forthrightness stems from a desire to protect individual political careers, now and in the future, and the Department's reputation, at the expense of learning all the facts and apportioning responsibility.

---

[150] SSCI Transcript, *Hearing on the Attacks in Benghazi,* November 15, 2012, p. 54 .
[151] *See* Jonathan Karl and Chris Good, "The Benghazi Emails: Talking Points Changed at State Dept.'s Request," *ABC News,* May 15, 2013, abcnews.go.com/Politics/Benghazi-emails-talking-points-changed-state-depts-request/story?id=19187137 (provides a link to the declassified and redacted emails at abcnews.go.com/images/Politics/white-house-benghazi-emails.pdf, p. 9).
[152] Ibid., p. 95.

Ironically, the State Department was not shy about voicing its concerns and objections to the Committee's draft report. In written comments, State made a concerted effort to downplay the Department's responsibility for ensuring the physical security of its employees and facilities overseas. For example, State repeatedly attempted to minimize its own culpability for the lack of security precautions by pointing to the fact that the same number of people died at the CIA Annex as at the Temporary Mission Facility and, therefore, CIA should be equally criticized for its own security at the Annex.[153] The logic is remarkable for its boldness, but neither helpful nor persuasive. The two security officers who were killed at the Annex were on the roof, in the act of defending the Annex, when they were struck by mortars. It is likely no amount of added physical security at the Annex would have prevented their deaths. Conversely, the Ambassador and Sean Smith were killed at the Temporary Mission Facility by attackers who easily gained unfettered access to the compound. There is a tremendous difference between a fortified facility that suffers a fatal blow from a mortar attack and a porous compound that yields to a basic ground assault. Yet, in an attempt to absolve itself of responsibility, State absurdly equated these scenarios. Moreover, this simplistic "numbers" argument fails to account for the likelihood that there would have been more American casualties, but for the successful rescue efforts by the Annex personnel.

Failures in Leadership—State Department

While many individuals with information relevant to our review were more than forthcoming with the Committee, we are particularly disappointed that Charlene Lamb, who was the Deputy Assistant Secretary for International Programs, has refused to explain to the Committee why certain decisions were made concerning enhanced security at the Temporary Mission Facility and who ultimately was responsible for those decisions. The Committee extended invitations to Ms. Lamb on three occasions prior to and after her reinstatement— each time, she refused to meet with the Committee.[154] Unfortunately, even after Ms. Lamb was returned to full duty, the State Department did not make her available to the Committee, something we believe should have been a priority for both Ms. Lamb and the State Department. Based on what we have learned during the Committee's review, we believe Ms. Lamb's testimony is critical to

---

[153] *"Intelligence Community Response, Fact-Based & Substantive Review Only Regarding SSCI Report of Terrorist Attacks on U.S. Facilities in Benghazi,"* August 30, 2013.
[154] The Committee extended invitations to Ms. Lamb through State on November 19, 2012, July 12, 2013, and August 20, 2013.

determining why the leadership failures in the State Department occurred and the specific extent to which these failures reached into its highest levels.

We know from the testimony of Eric Nordstrom, who served as the Regional Security Officer in Libya until shortly before the attacks, that Ms. Lamb and other senior State Department officials were unreceptive to repeated requests from the Libyan mission regarding security personnel in both Tripoli and Benghazi. According to Mr. Nordstrom, the previous U.S. Ambassador to Libya, Gene Cretz, and his Deputy Chief of Mission (DCM), Joan Polaschik, traveled to Washington in mid-February 2012 to specifically ask for additional security personnel.[155] In addition to meeting with Ms. Lamb, they met separately with Mr. Kennedy and other senior officials. Yet, when the Libyan mission transmitted its official request for additional security personnel on March 28, 2012, the pushback from Ms. Lamb's office was swift and significant. While the request, which included five temporary duty Diplomatic Security agents in Benghazi, was clearly reasonable, one of Ms. Lamb's subordinates asked Mr. Nordstrom why the official cable sought "the sun, the moon, and the stars." When Mr. Nordstrom stated that he did not understand why this was an issue, the response from Ms. Lamb's office was telling: "Well, you know, this is a political game. You have to not make us look bad here, that we're not being responsive."[156] In a disturbingly prophetic e-mail to DCM Polaschik following this exchange, Mr. Nordstrom wrote:

> I doubt we will ever get [Diplomatic Security] to admit in writing what I was told [in] reference [to] Benghazi that DI/[International Programs] was directed by Deputy Assistant Secretary Lamb to cap the agents in Benghazi at 3, and force post to hire local drivers. This is apparently a verbal policy only but one which DS/IP/[Near Eastern Affairs] doesn't plan to violate. I hope that nobody is injured as a result of an incident in Benghazi, since it would be particularly embarrassing to both DS and DAS [Lamb] if it was a result of some sort of game they are playing.[157]

According to Mr. Nordstrom, Ms. Lamb was also vocal about her unwillingness to provide additional security personnel, including support of an extension of the Department of Defense (DoD) Site Security Team. Mr.

---

[155] SSCI Transcript, *Member and Staff Interview of Eric Nordstrom*, June 27, 2013, pp. 5 and 26.
[156] Ibid., p. 28.
[157] *See* ibid., pp. 24-25.

Nordstrom told the Committee that Ms. Lamb claimed it would be embarrassing and give Libya more security agents than in Yemen and Pakistan.[158] In reality, as Mr. Nordstrom explained to both Ms. Lamb and the Committee, the Embassies in Sana'a and Islamabad actually complied with the Overseas Security Policy Board security standards and had security systems in place. On July 9, 2012, the Libyan mission sent another formal request for additional security personnel. The State Department never responded to this request in the form of a cable. According to Mr. Nordstrom, Ms. Lamb said that a response had been drafted, but was "lost in the shuffle."[159] Mr. Nordstrom's testimony does not stand alone. We heard of similar difficulties with Ms. Lamb from Gregory Hicks, the former DCM who arrived in Tripoli just over one month before the attacks. In a May 2012 briefing with Ms. Lamb as he prepared for his new assignment, he pushed back on the proposed security complement, but "did not get a favorable response" from Ms. Lamb.[160]

While Ms. Lamb should be held accountable for her actions in failing to provide better security in Benghazi, we believe that Mr. Kennedy, as the Under Secretary for Management, bears a specific responsibility for these lapses. According to DCM Hicks, the Libyan mission had a very unique status in that it was effectively on "ordered departure" status at all times. DCM Hicks also told the Committee that Mr. Kennedy approved every person who went to Libya and received a daily report on the number of personnel, their names, and their status.[161] Moreover, while Mr. Kennedy never responded to the Libyan mission's request for additional security personnel, he did specifically decline an offer from Lieutenant General Robert Neller, U.S. Marine Corps, Director of Operations, J3, the Joint Staff, to sustain or provide additional DoD security personnel in Libya by extending the deployment of the DoD Site Security Team in Tripoli, transitioning to a Marine Security Detachment, or deploying a U.S. Marine Corps Fleet Antiterrorism Security Team.[162] In short, he had direct insight into the security situation at all times, had received DoD offers of assistance, and affirmatively declined to improve the Libyan mission's security posture.

---

[158] Ibid., pp. 4 and 32.

[159] Ibid., p. 60.

[160] SSCI Transcript, *Member and Staff Interview of Gregory Hicks and Mark Thompson,* June 12, 2013, p. 10.

[161] SSCI Transcript, *Member and Staff Interview of Gregory Hicks,* June 19, 2013, p. 5.

[162] Email from Lieutenant General Robert B. Neller, U.S.M.C., JCS J3, to Patrick Kennedy, July 11, 2012, 2:46 PM; email from Patrick Kennedy to Lieutenant General Neller, July 13, 2012, 6:31 PM ("We are not/not requesting an extension of the team; and deeply appreciate the support we have had. We have finally been able to obtain weapons permits for the 11 new locally engaged Embassy bodyguards late last week and are in the process of integrating them into our operations.").

Ultimately, however, the final responsibility for security at diplomatic facilities lies with the former Secretary of State, Hillary Clinton. Because the Temporary Mission Facility in Benghazi did not meet the security standards set by the State Department, it would have required a waiver to be occupied. Although certain waivers of the standards could have been approved at a lower level, other departures, such as the co-location requirement, could only be approved by the Secretary of State.[163] At the end of the day, she was responsible for ensuring the safety of all Americans serving in our diplomatic facilities. Her failure to do so clearly made a difference in the lives of the four murdered Americans and their families.

The State Department's inordinate effort to minimize management failures contrasts sharply with its public commitment to accountability. At the same time, a strong case can be made that State engaged in retaliation against witnesses who were willing to speak with Congress. No reasonable explanation accounts for the State Department's unacceptable treatment of these witnesses, at the same time it returned to active duty witnesses such as Ms. Lamb who were shielded from, or actively avoided, Committee requests for interviews.

Failures in Leadership—General Dempsey

The failures in leadership relating to Benghazi were not limited to the State Department. The tenure of the Chairman of the Joint Chiefs of Staff, General Martin Dempsey, has been marked by what we view as significant deficiencies in command. From Syria to Benghazi, there has been either a profound inability or clear unwillingness to identify and prevent problems before they arise. Given the known operating environment in Benghazi, much less North Africa, a strong military leader would have ensured there was a viable plan in place to rescue Americans should the need arise. We understand the Department of Defense cannot plan for a rescue operation of every Embassy or diplomatic facility across the globe, but Benghazi was different given its hostile environment and lack of host nation security and support. Yet, there was no such plan. General Dempsey's attempts to excuse inaction by claiming that forces were not deployed because they would not have gotten there in time does not pass the common sense test. No one knew when the attacks against our facilities in Benghazi would end, or how aggressive the attacks would be. That is the whole point of a pre-established

---

[163] SSCI Transcript, *Member and Staff Interview of Eric Nordstrom,* June 27, 2013, pp. 36-37.

emergency rescue plan—so that the length of the attack alone does not dictate the rescue or survival of Americans. Understanding that the State Department bears ultimate responsibility for the safety of Americans serving in diplomatic facilities abroad, General Dempsey should have ensured that plan was in place, but he failed to do so.

A strong military leader would also have ensured that his commanders in the field were fully aware of all United States personnel, including CIA personnel, who were located within their areas of responsibility. Yet, the Committee has confirmed that General Carter Ham, as the Commander of U.S. Africa Command, was not even aware there was a CIA annex in Benghazi at the time of the attacks. We are puzzled as to how the military leadership expected to effectively respond and rescue Americans in the event of an emergency when it did not even know of the existence of one of the U.S. facilities. The fate of United States personnel serving in dangerous areas of the world should not rest on *ad hoc* rescue operations, no matter how heroic, simply because the United States Government and its civilian and military leaders have failed in their collective responsibilities to provide security and potentially life-saving assistance.

Continued Fall-out from No Detention Policy

As we learn from the errors and failures surrounding Benghazi, we believe one critical area of national security policy must be reexamined and changed by this Administration. President Obama and his Administration must end their efforts to close the detention facility at Guantanamo Bay and must develop a clear, cogent policy for the detention and interrogation of suspected terrorists. Since the President ordered Guantanamo's closure in 2009, we have witnessed a dangerous tendency to either not detain terrorism suspects or to conduct all-too-brief intelligence interrogations, followed by the inevitable reading of *Miranda* rights and appointment of counsel which often ends the interrogation. Amazingly, the same Administration that has demanded the closure of the state-of the-art detention facility at Guantanamo has vigorously embraced the use of floating prisons for conducting brief intelligence interrogations overseas. This approach is not only at odds with the spirit of the Geneva Conventions, but it fails to recognize how good intelligence collection can work if given the time to do so.

Intelligence collection and criminal prosecutions can work hand-in-hand, but we should not sacrifice intelligence collection simply because of the political unwillingness to detain a terrorist without criminal charges. Detaining and interrogating terrorism suspects—such as those believed to be involved in Benghazi—at Guantanamo Bay or other viable facilities outside the United States, as the law clearly provides, would ensure that we are maximizing the collection of vital intelligence, while still preserving the option to bring criminal charges. Instead, this Administration has chosen to return to a pre-9/11 mindset in which criminal charges take precedence over intelligence collection. As we saw with the 1998 Embassy bombings, the bombing of the USS Cole in 2000, and the September 11, 2001, terrorist attacks, this approach did not work then, and it does not work today. It is the perpetuation of this mindset that we believe is directly responsible for the Administration's failure to secure justice for those suspected of involvement in the attacks. If this Administration were serious about holding terrorists accountable for causing the deaths of American citizens, Khattala, al-Chalabi, and al-Harzi would today be at Guantanamo, instead of being free to continue to threaten Americans. We have heard the statistics about successful criminal prosecutions of terrorists; but at the end of the day, if we are not gathering the intelligence needed to prevent attacks and capture terrorists before they harm us, those statistics will neither help us protect this country nor provide much comfort to the families of those whose fate may be prematurely determined by terrorist attacks.

Aside from enabling key intelligence collection, long-term detention serves another invaluable function—it keeps dangerous terrorists behind bars. As the Committee's report notes, in the months leading up to the Benghazi terrorist attacks, the IC provided multiple warnings about terrorist activities in the region, including by al-Qa'ida and its affiliates. As press reports prior to and after the attacks indicate, there was particular concern about the rise of Ansar al-Sharia, the group involved in the Benghazi attacks that, according to public reports, was founded by former Guantanamo detainee Sufian bin Qumu.

Following the 2009 Executive order to close Guantanamo, there has been a concerted effort by this Administration to downplay the recidivist activities of former Guantanamo detainees in support of its overtly political goal to transfer as many detainees as possible to foreign countries and even to the United States. Listening to supporters of this ill-advised Executive order, one would believe that former detainees have universally rejected their terrorist associations and are now living peaceably throughout the world. The facts say otherwise. The recidivism rate among all former detainees is now over 29% and rising consistently. We know that al-Qa'ida in the Arabian Peninsula has counted former detainees among its leaders and members. Yet, the Administration continues to press for the release of more detainees, even to locations plagued by terrorism and amidst evidence that they will not be effectively monitored by host countries. Not every detainee must be held indefinitely, but not one should be released unless it is absolutely clear that he will no longer pose a threat to the United States or our interests. We simply cannot risk another Sufian bin Qumu being involved in terrorist activities that result in the deaths of American citizens.

Unanswered Questions

We believe the Committee's report has adequately reviewed and reported on the actions by the IC relating to Benghazi. Due to the issues outlined above, however, this review did not exhaust every question or provide every answer relating to these attacks. There remain important issues that should be addressed by congressional committees with express jurisdiction over these matters. It is our hope that the Committee's report and these Additional Views will assist in the eventual disclosure of those facts necessary to determine why our personnel and facilities in Benghazi were so vulnerable to attack. For example, we believe the issues of accountability and retaliation within the State Department must be fully explored by a committee that can and will use its subpoena authority to obtain information from an uncooperative State Department. It is wholly unsatisfactory that no one has borne responsibility for the poor policy decisions regarding the security of the Benghazi facility that appear to have been made at the highest levels of the Department. As we noted, the ultimate accountability lies with the former Secretary of State, and we believe there should be a full examination of her role in these events, including on the night of the attacks.

Questions also remain about who took the deployment of the Foreign Emergency Support Team (FEST) "off the table" and why this decision was made. The Committee has been told that this decision was made during a meeting that included Mr. Kennedy, the Secretary of State, and the Secretary of Defense. While we believe the military should have been the first response, the FEST's terrorism response mission—and previous deployments following the 1998 East Africa Embassy bombings and the 2000 USS Cole bombing, should have put them squarely in play. Yet, in what seems to be an unwillingness by State Department leadership to acknowledge that Benghazi was a terrorist incident, the decision was made to not deploy the FEST. The Committee interviewed Mark Thompson,

Deputy Coordinator for Operations at the State Department, who believed that the FEST option was taken off the table because of safety concerns. As Mr. Thompson testified before the Committee, this rationale did not make sense, given that the discussion was about sending the FEST to Tripoli or a nearby country, not to Benghazi.[164]

Similarly, there must be a full examination of our military response, or lack thereof. The CIA and other elements of the IC do, and must continue to, gather intelligence in dangerous areas of the world, as they did in Benghazi. Once they are asked to do so, however, we must do more to keep them safe. We appreciate that steps have been taken to ensure that U.S. assets can be deployed more quickly in the future, but the Benghazi families are entitled to understand the full facts surrounding response decisions made during the attacks. Only with the airing of these facts can supposition and conjecture be put to rest, and be replaced with full accountability.

Recently, new questions surfaced regarding the accuracy of information provided to Congress by the CIA about nondisclosure agreements signed by security officers who were present during the attacks. We have heard and understand the CIA's oral and written explanations for why these new agreements were needed, but are troubled by the lack of clarity in their initial response and the fact that this discrepancy had to be pointed out by personnel formerly associated with the CIA. As with other matters in this review, the Administration's lack of transparency and candor is raising more questions than the underlying discrepancy itself. At the same time, the Committee has learned that the CIA Inspector General did not investigate complaints relating to the Benghazi attacks from CIA whistleblowers. Whether these complaints are ultimately substantiated or dismissed is irrelevant. On a matter of this magnitude involving the deaths of four Americans, the Inspector General has a singular obligation to take seriously and fully investigate any allegation of wrongdoing. His failure to do so raises significant questions that we believe the Committee must explore more fully.

Finally, we believe the role of the White House must be fully explored. As we write these Additional Views, we are still without a full understanding of the substance of the Deputies Committee meeting that resulted in the final changes to the talking points, and we have yet to receive a clear explanation of the specific

---

[164] SSCI Transcript, *Member and Staff Interview of Gregory Hicks and Mark Thompson*, June 12, 2013, pp. 32 and 38.

interactions among the President, the Secretary of Defense, and the Secretary of State on the night of the attacks. This is not a call for Situation Room photos. It is a demand for the truth that is owed the American people.

Conclusion

The failures of Benghazi can be summed up this way: the Americans serving in Libya were vulnerable; the State Department knew they were vulnerable; and no one in the Administration really did anything about it. The Intelligence Community does not collect intelligence about threats to our security in dangerous place so it can be ignored by senior decisionmakers. Nor should a Regional Security Officer's repeated warnings go unheeded. Yet, the intelligence and warnings from the field were met by this Administration with a deafening silence. The four Americans who perished in Benghazi deserved better from their country. Their families, who have been waiting over a year for promised justice and answers, are entitled to know the truth about what happened and why. It is our intent that the findings and recommendations outlined in this report will facilitate and inform other reviews, especially those conducted by congressional committees with specific jurisdiction over the State Department. We stand ready to assist those reviews in every way possible. Ultimately, we must ensure that all the facts about our government's actions prior to, during, and after the attacks are brought to light for the American people to judge for themselves. The families of those murdered in Benghazi deserve the truth, and all of our intelligence, military, and diplomatic professionals who serve overseas in dangerous places are entitled to have confidence that the errors of Benghazi will not be repeated.

SAXBY CHAMBLISS
RICHARD BURR
JAMES E. RISCH
DAN COATS
MARCO RUBIO
TOM COBURN, M.D.

82

ADDITIONAL VIEWS OF SENATOR COLLINS

The Senate Select Committee on Intelligence (SSCI) "Review of Terrorist Attacks on U.S. Facilities in Benghazi, September 11-12, 2012," represents the most extensive review to date of the actions and analysis of the Intelligence Community (IC) leading up to, during, and after the attacks in Benghazi. I commend the SSCI leaders and staff for drafting a report that joins the only one other Senate report on Benghazi, "Flashing Red: A Special Report on the Terrorist Attack at Benghazi," an analysis that Joseph Lieberman, the former Chairman of the Senate Homeland Security and Governmental Affairs Committee (HSGAC), and I authored and issued in December 2012. Our Homeland Security Committee conducted the first bipartisan investigation of what took place during the terrorist attack that cost four Americans their lives. Although hampered by time constraints and insufficient cooperation by the Administration, our report is an indictment of the State Department's failure to adequately secure the Benghazi compound despite numerous indications of an extremely dangerous threat environment.

Like our report, the SSCI report joins an increasing number of analyses to reach the sobering verdict that the State Department could have and should have done much more to prepare for the terrorist attack in Benghazi. The critical findings of this and previous reports regarding the judgments, actions, and management processes at the Department of State beg for accountability, and yet, more than a year after the attack, no one has been held responsible for the critical management failures that contributed to the vulnerability of the American personnel and facilities in Benghazi.

The SSCI report, while adding considerably to our knowledge, would have been strengthened if it had placed greater emphasis on the lack of accountability for the broader management failures at the State Department. It would have been premature for earlier reports published in the months immediately following the attack, such as the Accountability Review Board and the "Flashing Red" report, to reach final judgments with respect to the State Department's personnel actions because the contributing factors to the vulnerability of the facility were still being pieced together. This report could have more fully evaluated the accountability issues because sufficient time had elapsed for the State Department to demonstrate whether or not decision-makers would be held accountable for poor judgments, refusals to tighten security, and misinformation.

For example, Under Secretary of State for Management Patrick Kennedy testified before the Homeland Security and Governmental Affairs Committee in 2012 that the threat environment in Benghazi was "flashing red," yet our investigation found that Under Secretary Kennedy, and other State Department officials, failed to ensure that a facility he personally approved in December 2011 had the necessary security to match the heightened threat environment.

The SSCI report describes many of the management deficiencies that contributed to the inadequate security posture: excessive confusion in the State Department's security decision-making process, uncertainty regarding the facility's future, and the absence of sufficient communication at State Department headquarters. As referenced in the report, the State Department Office of Inspector General (OIG) also found that the Department lacks a conceptual framework and process for risk management, and the Independent Best Practices panel found that security standards waivers for overseas facilities are commonplace. Of the 29 Accountability Review Board (ARB) recommendations, fully 26 relate to systemic management reforms in the Department according to the OIG.

Furthermore, this report, as well as other reports examining Benghazi, has found that the State Department failed to act upon some of the lessons learned from previous attacks. The State Department OIG's September 2013 audit of the ARB process listed four pages of recommendations by the Benghazi ARB that mirror similar recommendations from the report of the ARBs following the 1998 East Africa embassy bombings nearly fourteen years earlier. The OIG blamed this outcome, in part, on the absence of sustained oversight among Department principals, who are defined as the Secretary, deputy secretaries, and under secretaries.

A broken system overseen by senior leadership contributed to the vulnerability of U.S. diplomats and other American personnel in one of the most dangerous cities in the world. This is unacceptable, and yet the Secretary of State has not held anyone responsible for the system's failings. This leads to a perception that senior State Department officials are exempt from accountability because the Secretary of State has failed to hold anyone accountable for the systemic failures and management deficiencies that contributed to the grossly inadequate security for the Benghazi facility.

To be clear, the responsibility for the attack lies with the attackers themselves. Unfortunately, the promises of the President and other senior Administration officials to bring any of the attackers to justice have ringed hollow thus far. The report finds that more than a year after the attack, the terrorists who perpetrated the attack have still not been brought to justice.
The report includes an important recommendation I requested, in consultation with the Chairman and Vice Chairman, that the U.S. government must bring the attackers to justice in spite of the unwillingness or lack of capacity of the Libyan government to assist in this effort. Failure to do so would be to repeat one of the mistakes that contributed to the lethality of the attack, which was the excessive reliance on a local Libyan security force that lacked the capacity or willingness to defend the compound.

The failure to follow through on this promise undermines the credibility of the United States, diminishes the commitments made to the families who lost loved ones that night, and ignores the fact that our adversaries pay very close attention to our response to terrorist attacks. In general, inaction has not made the United States any safer. The failure of the United States to respond meaningfully, in the view of our adversaries, to attacks prior to 9/11/01, such as the 1998 al Qaeda attack against U.S. embassies in Kenya and Tanzania and the 2000 USS Cole bombing, served only to embolden the terrorists to plan and execute larger and more deadly attacks.

Finally, the report does not go far enough to address the Administration's failure to correctly label the incident as a deliberate and organized terrorist attack in the days following the attack. As our "Flashing Red" report found, there was never any doubt among key officials, including officials in the IC and the Department of State, that the attack in Benghazi was an act of terrorism. Yet, high-ranking Administration officials, including the President himself, repeatedly cast doubt on the nature of the attack, at times attributing it to the reaction to an anti-Islamic video and to a spontaneous demonstration that escalated into violence.

The SSCI report accurately describes that the IC moved too slowly to correct errors about a protest that never happened, and describes eyewitness testimony that should have been made available or pursued by the intelligence community more aggressively. The report does not, however, describe all of the operational reporting that should have been available to the IC after the attack.

85

12/31/19

Peter Navaro - U.S.

Nov 2016 Nov 9th predicted Dow 25K
in 4 yrs now Dow 28K
Predict Dow 31K in 2020.

GrownAmerican Superford.com